Q: Skills for Success

LISTENING AND SPEAKING

1

Teacher's Handbook

Jenni Currie Santamaria

OXFORD

UNIVERSITY PRESS

OXFORD
UNIVERSITY PRESS

198 Madison Avenue
New York, NY 10016 USA

Great Clarendon Street, Oxford OX2 6DP UK

Oxford University Press is a department of the University of Oxford.
It furthers the University's objective of excellence in research, scholarship,
and education by publishing worldwide in

Oxford New York

Auckland Cape Town Dar es Salaam Hong Kong Karachi
Kuala Lumpur Madrid Melbourne Mexico City Nairobi
New Delhi Shanghai Taipei Toronto

With offices in

Argentina Austria Brazil Chile Czech Republic France Greece
Guatemala Hungary Italy Japan Poland Portugal Singapore
South Korea Switzerland Thailand Turkey Ukraine Vietnam

OXFORD and OXFORD ENGLISH are registered trademarks of
Oxford University Press.

General Manager, American ELT: Laura Pearson
Publisher: Stephanie Karras
Associate Publishing Manager: Sharon Sargent
Associate Development Editor: Keyana Shaw
Director, ADP: Susan Sanguily
Executive Design Manager: Maj-Britt Hagsted
Associate Design Manager: Michael Steinhofer
Electronic Production Manager: Julie Armstrong
Production Artist: Elissa Santos
Cover Design: Michael Steinhofer
Production Coordinator: Elizabeth Matsumoto

ISBN: 978-0-19-475615-0 Listening and Speaking 1 Teacher's Handbook Pack
ISBN: 978-0-19-475658-7 Listening and Speaking 1 Teacher's Handbook
ISBN: 978-0-19-475664-8 Listening and Speaking 1 Testing Program CD-ROM

Printed in China

This book is printed on paper from certified and well-managed sources

10 9 8 7 6 5 4 3 2 1

ACKNOWLEDGMENTS

*The publishers would like to thank the following for their kind permission to reproduce
photographs:*
p. vi Marcin Krygier/iStockphoto; xiii Rüstem GÜRLER/iStockphoto

CONTENTS

WELCOME TO Q:Skills for Success

Q: Skills for Success is a six-level series with two strands, *Reading and Writing* and *Listening and Speaking*.

READING AND WRITING

LISTENING AND SPEAKING

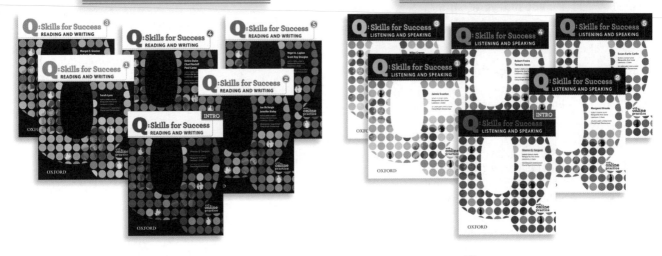

WITH Q ONLINE PRACTICE

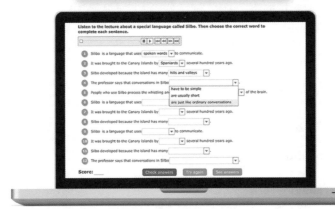

STUDENT AND TEACHER INFORMED

Q: Skills for Success is the result of an extensive development process involving thousands of teachers and hundreds of students around the world. Their views and opinions helped shape the content of the series. Q is grounded in teaching theory as well as real-world classroom practice, making it the most learner-centered series available.

To the Teacher
Highlights of the *Q: Skills for Success* Teacher's Handbook

LEARNING OUTCOMES

As you probably know from your own teaching experience, students want to know the point of a lesson. They want to know the "why" even when they understand the "how." In the classroom, the "why" is the learning outcome, and to be successful, students need to know it. The learning outcome provides a clear reason for classroom work and helps students meaningfully access new material.

Each unit in Oxford's *Q: Skills for Success* series builds around a thought-provoking question related to that unit's unique learning outcome. Students learn vocabulary to answer the unit question; consider new information related to the unit's theme that utilizes this vocabulary; use this information to think critically about new questions; and use those answers to practice the new listening, vocabulary, grammar, pronunciation, and speaking skills they need to achieve the unit's learning outcome.

Each aspect of the learning process in the Q series builds toward completing the learning outcome. This interconnected process of considering new information is at the heart of a critical thinking approach and forms the basis of the students' work in each unit of the Q series. At the end of the unit, students complete a practical project built around the learning outcome.

Learning outcomes create expectations in the classroom: expectations of what students will learn, what teachers will teach, and what lessons will focus on. Students benefit because they know they need to learn content for a purpose; teachers benefit because they can plan activities that reinforce the knowledge and skills students need to complete the learning outcome. In short, learning outcomes provide the focus that lessons need.

> In this example unit, students are asked to think about who makes them laugh while preparing to tell their own joke or funny story.

> The unit assignment ties into that unit's unique learning outcome.

UNIT 6
Unit QUESTION
Who makes you laugh?

Laughter

LISTENING • listening for specific information
VOCABULARY • synonyms
GRAMMAR • simple present for informal narratives
PRONUNCIATION • simple present third-person -s/-es
SPEAKING • using eye contact, pause, and tone of voice

LEARNING OUTCOME
Use appropriate eye contact, tone of voice, and pauses to tell a funny story or a joke to your classmates.

Tell a Story or Joke	20 points	15 points	10 points	0 points
Student told the joke or funny story easily (without long pauses or reading) and was easy to understand (spoke clearly and at a good speed).				
Student used the simple present tense correctly.				
Student used vocabulary from the unit.				
Student used eye contact, pauses, and tone of voice to effectively tell the joke or funny story.				
Student correctly pronounced third person -s/-es.				

Total points: _____
Comments:

> Clear assessments allow both teachers and students to comment on and measure learner outcomes.

Q Unit Assignment: Tell a joke or a funny story

Unit Question (5 minutes)

Refer students back to the ideas they discussed at the beginning of the unit about who makes them laugh. Cue students if necessary by asking specific questions about the content of the unit: *Why did people think Jackie Chan was funny? What advice did we hear about how to be funny? What skills can you use to make your jokes and stories more entertaining?*

Learning Outcome

1. Tie the Unit Assignment to the unit learning outcome. Say: *The outcome for this unit is to use appropriate eye contact, tone of voice, and pauses to tell a funny story or a joke to your classmates. This Unit Assignment is going to let you show that you can do that as well as correctly use and pronounce the simple present.*

v

CRITICAL THINKING

A critical thinking approach asks students to process new information and to learn how to apply that information to a new situation. Teachers might set learning outcomes to give students targets to hit—for example: "After this lesson, give three reasons why people immigrate"—and the materials and exercises in the lesson provide students with the knowledge and skills to think critically and discover *their* three reasons.

Questions are important catalysts in the critical thinking process. Questions encourage students to reflect on and apply their knowledge to new situations. Students and teachers work together to understand, analyze, synthesize, and evaluate the lesson's questions and content to reach the stated outcomes. As students become more familiar with these stages of the critical thinking process, they will be able to use new information to complete tasks more efficiently and in unique and meaningful ways.

Tip Critical Thinking

In Activity B, you have to **restate**, or say again in perhaps a different way, some of the information you learned in the two readings. **Restating** is a good way to review information.

B (10 minutes)

1. Introduce the Unit Question, *Why do people immigrate to other countries?* Ask related information questions or questions about personal experience to help students prepare for answering the more abstract unit question: *Did you immigrate to this country? What were your reasons for leaving your home country? What were your reasons for choosing your new country? What did you bring with you?*

2. Tell students: *Let's start off our discussion by listing reasons why people might immigrate. For example, we could start our list with finding work because many people look for jobs in new countries. But there are many other reasons why people immigrate. What else can we think of?*

Throughout the Student Book, *Critical Thinking Tips* accompany certain activities, helping students to practice and understand these critical thinking skills.

Critical Thinking Tip (1 minute)

1. Read the tip aloud.
2. Tell students that restating also helps to ensure that they have understood something correctly. After reading a new piece of information, they should try to restate it to a classmate who has also read the information, to ensure that they both have the same understanding of information.

The *Q Teacher's Handbook* features notes offering questions for expanded thought and discussion.

CRITICAL Q EXPANSION ACTIVITIES

The *Q Teacher's Handbook* expands on the critical thinking approach with the Critical Q Expansion Activities. These activities allow teachers to facilitate more practice for their students. The Critical Q Expansion Activities supplement the *Q Student Book* by expanding on skills and language students are practicing.

In today's classrooms, it's necessary that students have the ability to apply the skills they have learned to new situations with materials they have never seen before. *Q*'s focus on critical thinking and the *Q Teacher's Handbook's* emphasis on practicing critical thinking skills through the Critical Q Expansion Activities prepares students to excel in this important skill.

Critical Q: Expansion Activity

Outlining

1. Explain to students: *A popular way to prepare to outline one's ideas is to use a cluster map. In a cluster map, a big circle is drawn in the middle of a page or on the board, and a main point is written inside it—**this will become the topic sentence in the outline.***

2. Then explain: *Next, lines are drawn away from the circle and new, smaller circles are attached to the other end of those lines. Inside each of the smaller circles, ideas are written which relate to the main point—**these become supporting sentences in the outline.***

The easy-to-use activity suggestions increase student practice and success with critical thinking skills.

21ST CENTURY SKILLS

Both the academic and professional worlds are becoming increasingly interdependent. The toughest problems are solved only when looked at from multiple perspectives. Success in the 21st century requires more than just core academic knowledge—though that is still crucial. Now, successful students have to collaborate, innovate, adapt, be self-directed, be flexible, be creative, be tech-literate, practice teamwork, and be accountable—both individually and in groups.

Q approaches language learning in light of these important 21st Century Skills. Each unit asks students to practice many of these attributes, from collaboration to innovation to accountability, *while* they are learning new language and content. The Q *Student Books* focus on these increasingly important skills with unique team, pair, and individual activities. Additionally, the Q *Teacher's Handbooks* provide support with easy-to-use 21st Century Skill sections for teachers who want to incorporate skills like "openness to other people's ideas and opinions" into their classrooms but aren't sure where to start.

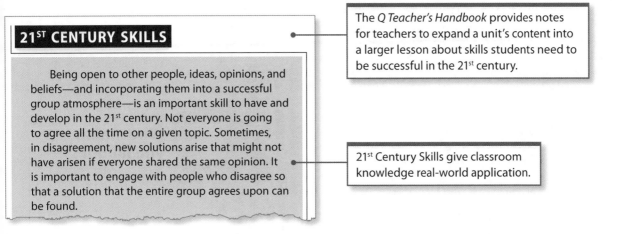

21ST CENTURY SKILLS

Being open to other people, ideas, opinions, and beliefs—and incorporating them into a successful group atmosphere—is an important skill to have and develop in the 21st century. Not everyone is going to agree all the time on a given topic. Sometimes, in disagreement, new solutions arise that might not have arisen if everyone shared the same opinion. It is important to engage with people who disagree so that a solution that the entire group agrees upon can be found.

The Q *Teacher's Handbook* provides notes for teachers to expand a unit's content into a larger lesson about skills students need to be successful in the 21st century.

21st Century Skills give classroom knowledge real-world application.

Q ONLINE PRACTICE

Q *Online Practice* is an online workbook that gives students quick access to all-new content in a range of additional practice activities. The interface is intuitive and user-friendly, allowing students to focus on enhancing their language skills.

For the teacher, Q *Online Practice* includes a digital grade book providing immediate and accurate assessment of each student's progress. Straightforward individual student or class reports can be viewed onscreen, printed, or exported, giving you comprehensive feedback on what students have mastered or where they need more help.

Teacher's Access Code Cards for the digital grade book are available upon adoption or for purchase. Use the access code to register for your Q *Online Practice* account at www.Qonlinepractice.com.

These features of the Q: *Skills for Success* series enable you to help your students develop the skills they need to succeed in their future academic and professional careers. By using learning outcomes, critical thinking, and 21st century skills, you help students gain a deeper knowledge of the material they are presented with, both in and out of the classroom.

Q connects critical thinking, language skills, and learning outcomes.

LANGUAGE SKILLS

Explicit skills instruction enables students to meet their academic and professional goals.

LEARNING OUTCOMES

Clearly identified **learning outcomes** focus students on the goal of their instruction.

UNIT 6

Laughter

LISTENING ● listening for specific information
VOCABULARY ● synonyms
GRAMMAR ● simple present for informal narratives
PRONUNCIATION ● simple present third-person -s/-es
SPEAKING ● using eye contact, pause, and tone of voice

LEARNING OUTCOME

Use appropriate eye contact, tone of voice, and pauses to tell a funny story or a joke to your classmates.

Unit QUESTION

Who makes you laugh?

PREVIEW THE UNIT

Ⓐ Discuss these questions with your classmates.

What funny movie or TV show do you like?
Do you tell jokes or make other people laugh?
Look at the photo. Do you think it is funny? Why or why not?

Ⓑ Discuss the Unit Question above with your classmates.

Listen to *The Q Classroom*, Track 16 on CD 2, to hear other answers.

102 UNIT 6

103

CRITICAL THINKING

Thought-provoking **unit questions** engage students with the topic and provide a **critical thinking framework** for the unit.

 Having the learning outcome is important because it gives students and teachers a clear idea of what the point of each task/activity in the unit is.
Lawrence Lawson, Palomar College, California

PREVIEW LISTENING 1

LANGUAGE SKILLS

Two listening texts provide input on the unit question and give **exposure to academic content.**

Jackie Chan—Action-Comedy Hero

You are going to listen to a radio program about Jackie Chan, a popular action-comedy film star. Look at the photos. Why do you think people will say Jackie Chan is funny? Give two reasons.

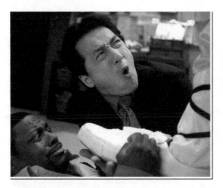

CRITICAL THINKING

Students **discuss** their opinions of each listening text and **analyze** how it changes their perspective on the unit question.

Q WHAT DO YOU THINK?

A. Discuss the questions in a group.

1. Do you agree that anyone can be funny? Why or why not?

2. Do you think Tate's advice is good? What other advice would you give to help people be funny?

3. What are favorite funny topics in your culture?

B. Think about both Listening 1 and Listening 2 as you discuss the questions.

1. How is the humor in a comedy film different than in a live theater? How are they the same?

 One of the best features is your focus on developing materials of a high "interest level."
Troy Hammond, Tokyo Gakugei University,
International Secondary School, Japan

Explicit skills instruction prepares students for academic success.

Q **WHAT DO YOU THINK?**

Discuss the questions in a group.

1. Why do people think Jackie Chan is funny? Do you think this type of sense of humor is funny?

2. Do you like *Kung Fu* or other similar movies? Why or why not?

3. Who are famous comedy stars from your country? Why do you think they are popular?

Listening Skill | **Listening for specific information**

Listening for specific information means listening for the important details you need. We listen for specific information especially when we listen to news or weather reports, transportation schedules, and instructions. Specific information includes details such as:

- names of people or places
- numbers, dates, or times (See Unit 5 Listening Skill, pages 87–88.)
- events

CD 2
Track 19

A. Read the information below. Then listen to Listening 1 again and write the missing information.

1. Jackie Chan's birth date: _____.

2. When he moved to Hollywood: _____.

3. What Americans thought of Chan in *Rush Hour*: _____.

4. Three reasons why he is funny:

    a. He smiles and _____.

    b. He's so _____.

    c. Fans love watching _____.

Speaking Skill | **Using eye contact, pause, and tone of voice**

When you tell a story or a joke, there are different ways to make it more interesting.

- **Make eye contact with the listener(s).** This will help you connect with your audience and keep them interested.
- **Use your voice to express different feelings.** This helps the listener understand the feelings of the people in the story.
- **Pause—stop speaking for a moment—**before you say the punch line (the end of a story or joke). This can help to make the ending a surprise.

CD 2
Track 25

Listen to the example.

...The man touches the rabbit, and the rabbit bites him.
"Ouch!" He says, "You said your rabbit doesn't bite!"
    surprised/angry tone of voice

The shopkeeper replies, "That isn't my rabbit!"
    ↑
    pause

CD 2
Track 26

A. Listen to the excerpts from the jokes. Underline the places where the speaker uses tone of voice. Draw an arrow (↑) where the speaker pauses.

1. One day, I'm at home. I turn on the TV and sit down on the sofa. My wife asks, "What are you doing?" I say, "Nothing." She says, "You did that yesterday." So I answer, "Yeah, I know. I wasn't finished."

2. The woman answers, "I hurt everywhere. It hurts when I touch my head. It hurts when I touch my leg, and it hurts when I touch my arm." The doctor thinks for a moment. Then he says, "I know what's wrong... Your finger is broken!"

B. Work with a partner. Read the excerpts from Activity A aloud. Practice making eye contact, using tone of voice, and pausing.

LEARNER CENTERED

Q Online Practice provides all new content for additional practice in an easy-to-use online workbook. Every student book includes a *Q Online Practice access code card.* Use the access code to register for your *Q Online Practice* account at www.Qonlinepractice.com.

Vocabulary Skill | **Synonyms** | web+

Synonyms are words that have almost the same or a similar meaning. The dictionary often gives synonyms in the definition of a word. In the examples, a synonym is given for *funny* while for *movie* only a definition is provided.

fun·ny 🔑 /ˈfʌni/ *adjective* (fun·ni·er, fun·ni·est)
1 making you laugh or smile: *a funny story* • *He's so funny!* ➲ **SYNONYM amusing**
2 strange or surprising: *There's a funny smell in this room.*

mov·ie 🔑 /ˈmuvi/ *noun*
1 [*count*] a story shown in moving pictures that you see in theaters or on television: *Would you like to **see a movie**?*

You can build your vocabulary by learning synonyms for words you already know. Learning synonyms will help you understand more when you listen.

All dictionary entries are taken from the *Oxford American Dictionary for learners of English.*

LANGUAGE SKILLS

A **research-based vocabulary program** focuses students on the words they need to know academically and professionally, using skill strategies based on the same research as the Oxford dictionaries.

All dictionary entries are taken from the *Oxford American Dictionary for learners of English.*

The *Oxford Basic American Dictionary for learners of English* was designed with English learners in mind, and provides extra learning tools for pronunciation, verb types, basic grammar structures, and more.

The Oxford 2000 Keywords 🔑
The Oxford 2000 Keywords encompasses the 2000 most important words to learn in English. It is based on a comprehensive analysis of the Oxford English Corpus, a two-billion word collection of English text, and on extensive research with both language and pedagogical experts.

The Academic Word List **AWL**
The Academic Word List was created by Averil Coxhead and contains **570 words that are commonly used in academic English**, such as in textbooks or articles across a wide range of academic subject areas. These words are a great place to start if you are studying English for academic purposes.

Clear learning outcomes focus students on the goals of instruction.

LEARNING OUTCOMES

A culminating unit assignment evaluates the students' **mastery of the learning outcome.**

Unit Assignment | Tell a joke or a funny story

 In this assignment, you are going to tell a funny story or joke to a group (or to the class). Use some of the tips from this unit to add interest and humor. Think about the question, "Who makes you laugh?" and refer to the Self-Assessment checklist on page 120 as you prepare to tell your joke or story.

For alternative unit assignments, see the *Q: Skills for Success Teacher's Handbook*.

CONSIDER THE IDEAS

Complete the tasks.

1. Read the joke and try to guess the punch line (the last line). Then listen to check your answer.

   A tourist visits Sydney, Australia. He wants to go to the beach. But he doesn't know how to get there. He sees a policeman. He waves to the policeman and says, "Excuse me! Can you help me?"

   The policeman comes over and says, "Yes, sir. How can I help you?"

   The tourist says, "Can you tell me the fastest way to get to the beach?"

LEARNER CENTERED

Track Your Success allows students to **assess their own progress** and provides guidance on remediation.

Check (✓) the skills you learned. If you need more work on a skill, refer to the page(s) in parentheses.

LISTENING	I can listen for specific information. (p. 107)
VOCABULARY	I can recognize and use synonyms. (p. 111)
GRAMMAR	I can recognize and use the simple present for informal narratives. (p. 113)
PRONUNCIATION	I can recognize and use the simple present third-person -s/-es. (p. 115)
SPEAKING	I can use eye contact, pause, and tone of voice. (p. 117)
LEARNING OUTCOME	I can use appropriate eye contact, tone of voice, and pauses to tell a funny story or a joke to my classmates.

 Students can check their learning ... and they can focus on the essential points when they study.

Suh Yoomi, Seoul, South Korea

Q Online Practice

For the student

- **Easy-to-use:** a simple interface allows students to focus on enhancing their speaking and listening skills, not learning a new software program
- **Flexible:** for use anywhere there's an Internet connection
- **Access code card:** a *Q Online Practice* access code is included with the student book. Use the access code to register for *Q Online Practice* at www.Qonlinepractice.com

For the teacher

- **Simple yet powerful:** automatically grades student exercises and tracks progress
- **Straightforward:** online management system to review, print, or export reports
- **Flexible:** for use in the classroom or easily assigned as homework
- **Access code card:** contact your sales rep for your *Q Online Practice* teacher's access code

Teacher Resources

Q Teacher's Handbook gives strategic support through:

- specific teaching notes for each activity
- ideas for ensuring student participation
- multilevel strategies and expansion activities
- the answer key
- special sections on 21st century skills and critical thinking
- a *Testing Program CD-ROM* with a customizable test for each unit

Oxford Teachers' Club

For additional resources visit the *Q: Skills for Success* companion website at www.oup.com/elt/teacher/Qskillsforsuccess

Q Class Audio includes:

- listening texts
- pronunciation presentations and exercises
- *The Q Classroom*

> It's an interesting, engaging series which provides plenty of materials that are easy to use in class, as well as instructionally promising.
> *Donald Weasenforth, Collin College, Texas*

SCOPE AND SEQUENCE   Listening and Speaking 1

UNIT	LISTENING	SPEAKING	VOCABULARY
1 Names **Q** **Do you like your name?** **LISTENING 1: Given Names and Nicknames** A Group Discussion (Cultural Anthropology) **LISTENING 2: Stage Names** A Radio Talk-Show (Linguistics)	• Predict content • Listen for main ideas • Listen for details • Listen for examples to better understand main ideas • Listen for reasons in order to understand a partner's background • Listen for sentence intonation to understand types of questions	• Take notes to prepare for a presentation or group discussion • Ask follow-up questions to keep a conversation going • Talk about reasons in order to explain your actions • Interview people to find out about their backgrounds	• Assess your prior knowledge of vocabulary • Prefixes that mean *not*
2 Work **Q** **How can you find a good job?** **LISTENING 1: Looking for a Job** An Online Job Search (Management) **LISTENING 2: The Right Person for the Job** A Job Interview (Human Resources)	• Predict content • Listen for main ideas • Listen for details • Understand key words and phrases to identify a topic • Listen for specific vocabulary items in context to figure out their meanings • Understand personal questions to describe yourself to an interviewer • Recognize word boundaries in a stream of speech to identify important vocabulary	• Take notes to prepare for a presentation or group discussion • Discuss qualities of applicants to determine the best for a job • Ask for repetition and clarification to make sure you understand • Role-play an interview to practice conversational skills and vocabulary use	• Assess your prior knowledge of vocabulary • Use a dictionary to distinguish between words with similar meanings
3 Long Distance **Q** **Why do we study other cultures?** **LISTENING 1: International Advertising** A Business Class Lecture (Anthropology) **LISTENING 2: Cultural Problems** Three Different Perspectives (Advertising)	• Predict content • Listen for main ideas • Listen for details • Practice listening to a lecture to identify problems mentioned by the speaker • Organize notes to show the structure of a passage • Identify individual words within sentences to understand key concepts • Listen for directions to understand what *should/ should not* be done	• Take notes to prepare for a presentation or group discussion • Work from notes to give a well-organized presentation • Maintain eye contact to keep a conversation partner engaged • Describe a personal experience to illustrate your cultural background	• Assess your prior knowledge of vocabulary • Use context to guess meanings of unfamiliar words

GRAMMAR	PRONUNCIATION	CRITICAL THINKING	UNIT OUTCOME
• Simple present statements and questions	• Intonation in *yes/no* and information questions	• Assess your prior knowledge of content • Relate personal experiences to listening topics • Integrate information from multiple sources • Reflect on what you have learned in the unit • Speculate about choices you might make • Recall personal histories • Appreciate formal and informal speaking situations	• Interview a classmate and introduce him/her to the class using the simple present tense
• Simple past • Regular and irregular verbs	• Past tense -*ed* endings	• Assess your prior knowledge of content • Relate personal experiences to listening topics • Integrate information from multiple sources • Reflect on what you have learned in the unit • Identify qualifications necessary for a task • Examine personal attributes and abilities • Assess personal preferences	• Write interview questions and role-play a job interview
• *Should/shouldn't* • *It's* + adjective + infinitive	• Reduced vowels (represented by the schwa /ə/ sound)	• Assess your prior knowledge of content • Relate personal experiences to listening topics • Integrate information from multiple sources • Reflect on what you have learned in the unit • Infer ideas from pictures • Compare and contrast cultures • Anticipate problems and suggest solutions	• Give a presentation about customs in a culture you know well

UNIT	LISTENING	SPEAKING	VOCABULARY
4 Positive Thinking **Q What makes a happy ending?** **LISTENING 1: A Bad Situation with a Happy Ending** A True Story (Psychology) **LISTENING 2: Make Your Own Happy Ending** A Radio Interview (Anthropology)	• Predict content • Listen for main ideas • Listen for details • Listen for reasons so you can better understand other people's beliefs • Apply questions like *who, what, when*, etc., to understand the basics of a story • Listen for syllable stress to recognize words in speech	• Take notes to prepare for a presentation or group discussion • Use expressions of interest to keep a conversation going • Organize information for a discussion • Use reasons to explain personal beliefs	• Assess your prior knowledge of vocabulary • Use a dictionary to find parts of speech
5 Vacation Time **Q What is the best kind of vacation?** **LISTENING 1: Places In Danger** A Podcast of a Travel Program (Ecology) **LISTENING 2: A Helpful Vacation** A Presentation about Volunteer Jobs (Hospitality and Tourism)	• Predict content • Listen for main ideas • Listen for details • Recognize numbers and dates to understand specific details • Take notes to identify support for main ideas • Recognize reduced forms to understand informal speech • Sort facts into categories to see content relationships	• Take notes to prepare for a presentation or group discussion • Use structure signals to introduce topics in a presentation • Ask follow-up questions to keep a conversation going • Express reasons to justify personal choices	• Assess your prior knowledge of vocabulary • Use the suffixes *-ful* and *-ing* to form adjectives
6 Laughter **Q Who makes you laugh?** **LISTENING 1: Jackie Chan—Action-Comedy Hero** A Radio Program (Film Study) **LISTENING 2: Can Anyone Be Funny?** A TV Interview (Psychology)	• Predict content • Listen for main ideas • Listen for details • Listen for exact words or phrases to improve your word recognition • Recognize sequence words to understand a flow of ideas • Listen for names and numbers to understand details in a passage • Recognize jokes to understand a speaker's intent	• Take notes to prepare for a presentation or group discussion • Use eye contact, pauses, and tone of voice to relate well to an audience • Include jokes or funny stories to make a presentation more interesting • Use narrative present verbs to create an informal tone	• Assess your prior knowledge of vocabulary • Use synonyms to give variety to speech
7 Music **Q Why is music important to you?** **LISTENING 1: Mind, Body, and Music** A University Lecture (Physiology) **LISTENING 2: Music in Our Lives** A Discussion (Psychology)	• Predict content • Listen for main ideas • Listen for details • Listen for enumeration signals to understand the structure of a passage • Understand answers in an interview to learn about someone's tastes and preferences • Listen for opinions to understand someone's attitudes and tastes	• Take notes to prepare for a presentation or group discussion • Ask follow-up questions to keep a conversation going • Converse politely, express your tastes and preferences, and ask about someone else's • Talk about musical tastes • Conduct an interview to practice asking questions about choice	• Assess your prior knowledge of vocabulary • Use the dictionary to find the correct definition of a word with several meanings

GRAMMAR	PRONUNCIATION	CRITICAL THINKING	UNIT OUTCOME
• *Because* and *so*	• Word stress of multi-syllable nouns	• Assess your prior knowledge of content • Relate personal experiences to listening topics • Integrate information from multiple sources • Reflect on what you have learned in the unit • Analyze your attitudes toward culture-based beliefs • Evaluate choices made by others • Combine information from multiple sources	• Participate in a group discussion about bad situations with happy endings.
• Future expressions with *be going to*	• Reduction of *be going to*	• Assess your prior knowledge of content • Relate personal experiences to listening topics • Integrate information from multiple sources • Reflect on what you have learned in the unit • Interpret photographs • Relate your own background to that of others • Assess personal preferences	• Give a presentation describing a tour to a popular travel destination
• Simple present verbs in narratives	• The 3rd person *-s* ending for simple present verbs	• Assess your prior knowledge of content • Relate personal experiences to listening topics • Integrate information from multiple sources • Reflect on what you have learned in the unit • Examine personal tastes • Evaluate the effectiveness of advice • Speculate about a possible career	• Use appropriate eye contact, tone of voice, and pauses to tell a funny story or a joke to your classmates
• Gerunds as subjects or objects	• Intonation in questions about choices	• Assess your prior knowledge of content • Relate personal experiences to listening topics • Integrate information from multiple sources • Reflect on what you have learned in the unit • Assess personal tastes and habits • Infer ideas from pictures • Classify musical pieces • Select culturally acceptable expressions of opinion	• Participate in a group interview asking and answering questions about how important music is in your lives

UNIT	LISTENING	SPEAKING	VOCABULARY
8 Honesty **Q** **When is honesty important?** **LISTENING 1: Dishonesty In Schools** A TV News Report (Criminology) **LISTENING 2: What's the Right Thing to Do?** Three Conversations (Sociology)	• Predict content • Listen for main ideas • Listen for details • Make inferences to understand a speaker's attitudes • Listen to identify methods of cheating in various circumstances • Listen for numbers to understand percentages and fractions • Identify individual words in rapid speech to improve listening precision	• Take notes to prepare for a presentation or group discussion • Credit sources to identify where information came from • Compose questions and organize them into a survey • Report results of a survey	• Assess your prior knowledge of vocabulary • Understand and use numbers to express percentages and fractions
9 Life Changes **Q** **Is it ever too late to change?** **LISTENING 1: Attitudes about Change** A Group Discussion (Psychology) **LISTENING 2: Tips from a Life Coach** A Radio Call-In Show (Language Studies)	• Predict content • Listen for main ideas • Listen for details • Listen for agreement / disagreement signals to understand opinions • Recognize indirect disagreement to understand a speaker's attitudes • Listen for exact words or phrases to improve your word recognition • Listen for statements of advice to determine what the speaker recommends • Identify individual words to precisely complete statements	• Take notes to prepare for a presentation or group discussion • Use questions to find out whether a listener understands you • Use agreement / disagreement signals to state your opinion • Use target vocabulary to give advice • Explain a sequence of events	• Assess your prior knowledge of vocabulary • Collocations of verbs and nouns
10 Fear **Q** **When is it good to be afraid?** **LISTENING 1: The Science of Fear** A Conference Presentation (Cognitive Psychology) **LISTENING 2: What Are You Afraid of?** A Discussion with a Doctor (Physiology)	• Predict content • Listen for main ideas • Listen for details • Take notes to reflect classifications made in a listening passage • Listen for examples to sort into classifications • Listen for cause-effect relationships in a presentation	• Take notes to prepare for a presentation or group discussion • Show surprise, happiness, and sadness in conversation • Tell a personal story to express fears • Role-play conversations to practice appropriate responses	• Assess your prior knowledge of vocabulary • Idioms and expressions

GRAMMAR	PRONUNCIATION	CRITICAL THINKING	UNIT OUTCOME
• Conjunctions *and* and *but*	• Linkages of consonants to vowels	• Assess your prior knowledge of content • Relate personal experiences to listening topics • Integrate information from multiple sources • Reflect on what you have learned in the unit • Rank actions as right or wrong • Relate personal experience to a topic • Recognize which source deserves credit for information	• Conduct a survey to gather opinions on honesty and dishonesty, and then report your results to the class
• Imperative of *Be* + adjective	• Content word stress in sentences	• Assess your prior knowledge of content • Relate personal experiences to listening topics • Integrate information from multiple sources • Reflect on what you have learned in the unit • Identify personal experiences relevant to a topic • Assess personal reactions to change • Speculate about future circumstances • Examine cultural values	• Deliver a presentation providing instructions on how a person can make a change in his/her life
• *So* and *such* with adjectives	• Linking vowel sounds with /w/ or /y/	• Assess your prior knowledge of content • Relate personal experiences to listening topics • Integrate information from multiple sources • Reflect on what you have learned in the unit • Recognize personal emotions • Analyze photographs • Infer a speaker's attitudes	• Use phrases for expressing emotions to describe a frightening experience

Unit QUESTION

Do you like your name?

Names

LISTENING • listening for examples
VOCABULARY • prefixes that mean *not*
GRAMMAR • simple present statements and questions
PRONUNCIATION • intonation in questions
SPEAKING • asking follow-up questions

LEARNING OUTCOME

Interview a classmate and introduce him/her to the class using the simple present tense.

▶ *Listening and Speaking 1, pages 2–3*

Preview the Unit

Learning Outcome

1. Ask for a volunteer to read the unit skills, then the unit learning outcome.

2. Explain: *This is what you are expected to be able to do by the unit's end. The learning outcome explains how you are going to be evaluated. With this outcome in mind, you should focus on learning these skills (Listening, Vocabulary, Grammar, Pronunciation, Speaking) that will support your goal of interviewing a classmate and introducing him/her to the class. These skills can also help you act as mentors in the classroom to help the other students meet this outcome.*

A (10 minutes)

1. To help students begin thinking about the topic, tell them your full name and any anecdotes you know about your name (e.g., why you were given your name, whether it's a common/popular name, how you feel about your name).

2. Put students in pairs or small groups to discuss the first two questions.

3. Call on volunteers to share their ideas with the class. Ask questions: *Is your name popular in your country? Are you named after someone? Do you have a nickname?*

4. Focus students' attention on the photo. Have a volunteer describe the photo to the class. Read the third question aloud. Ask students to call out names they know. Elicit whether the names are for males or females. Ask which names students like and why they like them.

Activity A Answers, p. 3
1. Answers may include first, middle, or family names.
2. Answers may include a shortened name, a nickname, a given name, or a last name.
3. Students may recognize Faith, Grace, and Gray but may not have known that they were names.

B (15 minutes)

1. Explain that each unit in Q focuses on a Unit Question that students will consider throughout the unit and will address in their Unit Assignment at the end.

2. Read the Unit Question aloud. Give students a minute to silently consider their answers. Then ask students who answered *yes* to stand on one side of the room and students who answered *no* to stand on the other side of the room. If all students stand on the *yes* side, try dividing them this way: *Stand on the right side if you prefer your last name and on the left side if you prefer your first name.*

3. Direct students to tell a partner next to them their reasons for choosing the side they did.

4. Call on volunteers to share their ideas.

5. Ask students to sit down, copy the Unit Question, and note their answers and reasons. They will refer back to the notes at the end of the unit.

Activity B Answers, p. 3
Possible answers: Lower-level students may answer with a simple *yes* or *no*. Mid-level students can expand with a brief explanation: *It's my grandfather's name* or *It's not pretty*. Higher-level students can provide an anecdote explaining their feelings: *My name is a tradition in my family that I'm proud of* or *People always spell my name wrong, and I get tired of spelling it all the time.*

EXPANSION ACTIVITY: Share Favorites (5 minutes)

1. Have students think about names they like.

2. Write questions on the board. *Why do you like the name? Does it have a special meaning? Is it common or unusual? Do you know anyone with the name?*

3. Have partners use the questions to discuss names they like. Then ask volunteers to share their ideas with the class.

The Q Classroom

🔊 CD1, Track 2

1. Explain to students that they are going to hear a teacher and several students discuss the Unit Question. Ask them to listen for how many students there are and to try to catch their names.

2. Play the Q Classroom. Elicit the names of the Q Classroom students: *Yuna, Sophy, Marcus,* and *Felix.* Replay the audio and ask specific questions: *Who was Yuna named for? Is her name common in Korea? Why did Sophy's parents choose her name? What problem does she have with her name? Why does Marcus like his name? What does Felix's name mean? What problem does he have with his name?*

▶ *Listening and Speaking 1, page 4*

C (5 minutes)

1. Direct partners to read the introductions.

2. Write sentence frames on the board to support lower-level students: *My friends call me _____ because _____ . _____ is short for _____ . I don't have a nickname.* Then have students introduce themselves to their partners.

D (10 minutes)

1. Have each pair sit with another pair and repeat the introduction process.

2. Read the chart headings and the information about Liz and Janek. Tell students to complete the chart with their group members' information. Put questions on the board for them to ask if they need to clarify: *What was your nickname again? How do you spell your given name?*

E (10 minutes)

1. Assign roles to the students in each group: a group leader to make sure everyone contributes, a note-taker to record the group's ideas, a reporter to share the group's ideas with the class, and a timekeeper to watch the clock.

2. Have students discuss the questions. Call on the reporter from each group to share the group's answers. Discuss how many students have names that are common.

Critical Q: Expansion Activity

Compare Information

Students can deepen their understanding of newly acquired information by comparing it with information they already know. Practice this useful strategy with this activity.

For question 2, make a chart on the board like the one below, using students' countries. Ask students to make comparisons among the words. Are any of the words similar? In what way? Have students compare the words in terms of length (normally shorter than the formal word), sound (many of them use *b*, *d*, *n*, and *m*, which are easy sounds for babies to pronounce), and formation (in some languages, a general diminutive is applied, as in *Abuelito*, which adds the diminutive *ito* to the word for *grandfather*).

	U.S.	Mexico
mother	Mom, Mommy	Mamá
father	Dad, Daddy	Papá
grandmother	Grandma	Abuelita
grandfather	Grandpa	Abuelito

LISTENING

▶ *Listening and Speaking 1, page 5*

LISTENING 1: Given Names and Nicknames

VOCABULARY (15 minutes)

1. Put students in pairs to read the sentences and definitions and circle the definitions for the bold words.

2. Elicit the answers and write the letters on the board. Then go over each sentence, discussing the vocabulary words. Elicit the part of speech and use the word in a new example or context. For example: *Is* **opinion** *a noun or a verb? What is your* **opinion** *about your name?*

> **Vocabulary Answers, p. 5**
> **1.** a; **2.** b; **3.** b; **4.** a; **5.** a; **6.** b

Tip for Success (5 minutes)

1. Read the tip aloud. Discuss different ways of organizing a vocabulary notebook. Students can create alphabetical or part-of-speech sections, or they can divide their notebook into the ten units of the book and record the words they learn in each unit.

2. Also discuss the best information to put in a vocabulary notebook. In addition to the part of speech and a brief definition or translation, students should include an example sentence with each word to help them remember it.

3. Demonstrate sentences that work as useful memory aids vs. those that don't. For example, *In my opinion, _____ is a good movie* is a useful memory aid because it has personal meaning for the student and contains a clue to the definition. In contrast, *I have many opinions* isn't a useful sentence because the vocabulary word could be substituted with many other nouns.

 For additional practice with the vocabulary, have students visit *Q Online Practice*.

▶ *Listening and Speaking 1, page 6*
PREVIEW LISTENING 1 (3–5 minutes)

1. Direct students to look at the photos. Ask: *Where are they? What are they wearing? Who do you think they are?*

2. Have students answer the question. Tell them they should review their answers after listening.

> **Preview Listening 1 Answers, p. 6**
> **1.** given names; **2.** nicknames

Listening 1 Background Note

The most common nicknames, like the ones mentioned in Listening 1, are shortened forms of given names. Additional examples include: (English) Jenny for Jennifer, Phil for Philip, (Spanish) Paco for Francisco, Lupe for Guadalupe, (Japanese) Kimutaku for Kimura Takuya, (Russian) Sasha for Alexander or Alexandra.

However, there are many other kinds of nicknames that are usually only used by close friends and family, particularly for children (Princess). Nicknames based on occupation (Doc) or birthplace (Tex) are also fairly common. It should be noted that nicknames based on physical attributes, although they may be fine in other languages, e.g., Flaco (skinny) in Spanish, are normally insulting in English.

LISTEN FOR MAIN IDEAS (5 minutes)

 CD1, Track 3

1. Direct students to read the sentences before they listen. Explain that they should check only the main, or most important, ideas.

2. Play the audio and have students complete the activity individually.

3. Elicit the answers from the class. Point out that all of the main ideas talk about how your name affects the way people view you.

> **Listen for Main Ideas Answers, p. 6**
> Checked: 2, 3

LISTEN FOR DETAILS (10 minutes)

 CD1, Track 4

1. Direct students to read the statements before they listen again.

2. As you play the audio, have students listen and circle the correct word.

3. Have students compare answers with a partner.

4. Replay the audio so that the partners can check their answers.

5. Go over the answers with the class.

Listen for Details Answers, p. 6
1. honest; **2.** successful; **3.** popular

 For additional practice with listening comprehension, have students visit *Q Online Practice*.

▶ *Listening and Speaking 1, page 7*

WHAT DO YOU THINK? (10 minutes)

1. Ask students to read the questions and reflect on their answers.

2. Seat students in small groups and assign roles: a group leader to make sure everyone contributes, a note-taker to record the group's ideas, a reporter to share the group's ideas with the class, and a timekeeper to watch the clock.

3. Give students five minutes to discuss the questions. Call time if conversations are winding down. Allow them an extra minute or two if necessary.

4. Call on each group's reporter to share ideas with the class.

What Do You Think? Answers, p. 7
Possible answers:
1. Students can say which name they use at school, at work, at home, and in the community.
2. People might expect someone whose name is unusual/old-fashioned/modern, etc., to have a personality to match, or they might have preconceptions about someone based on other people they've known with the same name.
3. People think differently about you depending on what name you give them; people connect names with personalities; if you use your given name, people think you're honest.

Learning Outcome

Use the learning outcome to frame the purpose and relevance of Listening 1. Ask: *What did you learn from Listening 1 that prepares you to interview a classmate and introduce him/her to the class?* (Students learned about given names and nicknames. They can ask their classmates about their given names and nicknames and where they use each name.)

Listening Skill: Listening for examples (5 minutes)

1. Direct students to read the information silently.

2. Check comprehension by asking questions: *Which expressions can come in the middle of a sentence? (all three) Which can begin a sentence? (for example) Where do the commas go for* such as? like? for example?

3. Refer to the 21st Century Skills box on page 6 for more ideas on teaching listening for examples.

A (5 minutes)
CD1, Track 5

1. Play the audio and have students complete the sentences.

2. Call on volunteers to read the completed sentences aloud.

Activity A Answers, pp. 7–8
1. such as; **2.** like; **3.** for example; **4.** such as

▶ *Listening and Speaking 1, page 8*

B (10 minutes)
CD1, Track 6

1. Direct students to work with a partner to complete the sentences with words from the box. Play the audio and have partners check their answers.

2. Ask students to point out the markers used to introduce examples. Have partners read the conversation.

Activity B Answers, p. 8
1. nickname;
2. opinion;
3. introduce;
4. differently;
5. honest;
6. honest;
7. successful;
8. popular

 For additional practice with listening for examples, have students visit *Q Online Practice*.

In any situation that requires understanding an extended presentation, whether in the classroom or in the workplace, students need to pick up on markers that signal the speaker's intentions. This skill is especially useful in students' future academic and professional careers, where they will likely spend significant amounts of time listening to lectures, workplace training sessions, and colleagues' presentations. This unit focuses on listening for examples to help students become aware of expressions speakers use to tell their listeners that they're about to hear an example (*like*, *such as*, and *for example*).

To support this skill, become conscious of your own use of these markers and draw students' attention to your use of them. For extra practice, give a short "lecture" and ask students to raise their hands every time they hear one of the expressions.

Tip for Success (1 minute)

1. Read the tip aloud.
2. Encourage students to monitor each other's use of the expressions *like*, *such as*, and *for example*.

▶ *Listening and Speaking 1, page 9*

LISTENING 2: Stage Names

VOCABULARY (10 minutes)

1. Direct students to read the words and definitions in the box. Pronounce the words and have students repeat them.
2. Have students work with a partner to complete the conversations. Call on volunteers to read the conversations aloud.
3. Have the pairs read each conversation together.

> **Vocabulary Answers, p. 9**
> **1.** pronounce;   **2.** unusual;   **3.** ordinary;
> **4.** famous;   **5.** similar;   **6.** choose

 For additional practice with the vocabulary, have students visit *Q Online Practice*.

▶ *Listening and Speaking 1, page 10*

PREVIEW LISTENING 2 (3–5 minutes)

1. Direct students' attention to the photos and ask: *Do you recognize these people? What does he/she do? Do you like his/her music/movies? These names are "stage names." What do you think a "stage name" is?*
2. Have students match the real names to the stage names. Tell them they should review their answers after the listening.

> **Preview Listening 2 Answers, p. 10**
> 3, 1, 2

Listening 2 Background Note

Ringo Starr was the drummer for the Beatles from 1962 to 1970. He also sang several of the band's popular songs, including, "With a Little Help from my Friends" and "Yellow Submarine."

Miley Cyrus is a pop singer who became famous after starring in the Disney Channel series *Hannah Montana*. She was 12 years old when she landed the starring role on the show and 15 when she released her first solo CD.

Bruce Lee was born in San Francisco but raised in Hong Kong. He appeared in more than 25 movies, and his films brought martial-arts movies to a new level of international popularity. He died in 1973.

Critical Thinking Tip (1 minute)

1. Read the tip aloud.
2. Explain to students that when they match two things, they are looking for information that goes together.

LISTEN FOR MAIN IDEAS (5 minutes)

CD1, Track 7

1. Direct students to read all of the reasons. Ask them to guess which reasons they think they will hear. Ask them which reasons seem unlikely.
2. Play the audio and have students complete the activity individually.
3. Call on volunteers for the answers.

> **Listen for Main Ideas Answers, p. 10**
> Checked: 2, 3, 5

LISTEN FOR DETAILS (5–10 minutes)

 CD1, Track 8

1. Direct students to read the questions and answer choices before they listen again.

2. As you play the audio, have students listen and circle the correct answers.

3. Have students compare answers with a partner.

4. Replay the audio so that partners can check their answers.

5. Go over the answers with the class.

> **Listen for Details Answers, p. 11**
> **1.** c; **2.** a; **3.** a; **4.** b; **5.** a

For additional practice with listening comprehension, have students visit *Q Online Practice*.

WHAT DO YOU THINK?

A (10 minutes)

1. Ask students to read the questions and reflect on their answers.

2. Seat students in small groups and assign roles: a group leader to make sure everyone contributes, a note-taker to record the group's ideas, a reporter to share the group's ideas with the class, and a timekeeper to watch the clock.

3. Give students five minutes to discuss the questions. Call time if conversations are winding down. Allow them an extra minute or two if necessary.

4. Call on each group's reporter to share ideas with the class.

> **Activity A Answers, p. 12**
> Possible answers:
> **1.** marriage, to fit in in a new country, because their name is too unusual;
> **2.** Students may not want to change their names because they like them or because it would be complicated; students may want to change their names because they don't like them or because they're difficult to pronounce.

B (5 minutes)

1. Keep students in their small groups and ask them to discuss the questions in Activity B.

Tell them to choose a new leader, note-taker, reporter, and timekeeper.

2. Call on the new reporter to share the group's answers to the questions.

Learning Outcome

Use the learning outcome to frame the purpose and relevance of Listenings 1 and 2. Ask: *What did you learn from Listenings 1 and 2 that prepares you to interview a classmate and introduce him/her to the class?* (Students learned why some people use names that are different than their given names. They can ask their classmates about why they use their nicknames instead of their given names.)

Vocabulary Skill: Prefixes that mean *not* (3–5 minutes)

1. Direct students to read the information in the box.

2. Check comprehension: *What does* dislike *mean?* Use the *dis-* prefix with familiar words and ask students to guess the meaning: *What do you think* disrespect *means? Do the same with the prefixes* in- *and* un-. *What does* informal *mean? What do you think* invisible *means? What does* unusual *mean? What do you think* unnecessary *means?*

Skill Note

Learning prefixes is an important part of vocabulary development. Make an effort to point out *in-*, *dis-*, and *un-* in words to increase students' awareness.

Some other common words with these prefixes: *discontinue, disappear, disconnect; unsafe, unclean, unfinished, unknown; incapable, incomplete.*

The prefix *in-* becomes *il-* when placed in front of root words beginning with *l* (*illegal*) and becomes *im-* when placed in front of root words beginning with *m* or *p* (*immoral, impossible*).

A (5 minutes)

1. Direct students to look up *active* in the dictionary and find where *inactive* is listed as the antonym. Explain what an antonym is. Have students work individually to complete the chart.

2. Go over the answers with the class. Answer any questions about meaning.

> **Activity A Answers, p. 12**
> inactive, disagree, inconvenient, incorrect, inexpensive, unfriendly, dishonest, unpopular

▶ *Listening and Speaking 1, page 13*

B (10 minutes)

1. Direct students to work individually to complete the conversations.

2. Have students compare answers with a partner. Then ask the pairs to read each conversation.

3. Call on volunteer pairs to read them aloud.

> **Activity B Answers, p. 13**
> **1.** incorrect; **2.** disagree; **3.** inconvenient;
> **4.** unusual; **5.** inactive; **6.** inexpensive;
> **7.** unfriendly; **8.** dishonest

 For additional practice with prefixes that mean *not*, have students visit *Q Online Practice*.

▶ *Listening and Speaking 1, pages 14–15*

SPEAKING

Grammar Part 1: Simple present statements (10 minutes)

1. Read the statements and examples about when the simple present is used. Provide and elicit additional examples for each situation. For example, general truths: *Some names are very unusual. Parents choose names for many different reasons.* Habits: *He studies at the library. She calls her friends by their nicknames.* States and feelings: *I am tired. She has long hair.*

2. Focus students' attention on the charts. Say and have students repeat the sentences.

3. Check comprehension by having volunteers make affirmative and negative first-person statements: *I am from Mexico. I don't like cold weather.* Then ask other students to make statements about their classmates: *Jorge is from Mexico. He doesn't like cold weather.*

Skill Note

Use these tips to help students focus on subject-verb agreement for third-person singular. Before they read a passage or an exercise aloud, point out the third-person singular verbs and have them underline the *s* so they remember to pronounce it. Before they turn in a piece of writing, direct them to review each verb to determine whether it is present tense third-person singular. When they are speaking, make a note when they drop the final *s*, and ask them to repeat their ideas, pronouncing the verb form correctly.

A (5 minutes)

1. Direct students to read the sentences and circle the correct verbs.

2. Call on volunteers to read the sentences aloud.

> **Activity A Answers, p. 15**
> **1.** are; **2.** have, use; **3.** is, calls;
> **4.** don't, get; **5.** doesn't, thinks; **6.** isn't, It's

▶ *Listening and Speaking 1, page 16*

B (5–10 minutes)

1. Direct students to work individually to complete the sentences.

2. Have students compare answers with a partner and read the paragraph aloud. Remind them to pronounce the third-person *s*.

3. Call on volunteers to read the paragraph aloud.

> **MULTILEVEL OPTION:**
>
> Pair students of similar levels. Provide lower-level pairs with a word bank to help them complete the activity. Ask higher-level students to write sentences about themselves and their families using the exercise as a model. Have them read their completed sentences to their partners. After you have corrected the exercise as a class, call on higher-level volunteers to read the sentences they wrote.

> **Activity B Answers, p. 16**
> **1.** is; **2.** don't have; **3.** isn't;
> **4.** means; **5.** am; **6.** have;
> **7.** live; **8.** doesn't live; **9.** has;
> **10.** works; **11.** is; **12.** doesn't like;
> **13.** call; **14.** likes; **15.** doesn't have

 For additional practice with simple present statements, have students visit *Q Online Practice*.

▶ *Listening and Speaking 1, pages 16–17*

Grammar Part 2: Simple present questions (5 minutes)

1. Focus students' attention on the charts. Say and have students repeat the *yes/no* and information questions. Using statements from Part 1, show students how a statement becomes a question.

2. Check comprehension. Ask questions: *With regular verbs, do we use the s form in the question? When do we use* do *or* does?

A (5 minutes)

1. Direct students to work individually to unscramble the questions.

2. Have students compare answers with a partner.

3. Call on volunteers to read the questions to the class.

Activity A Answers, p. 17
2. Who is your favorite actor?
3. Where does your sister work?
4. Is it impolite to use your nickname at work?
5. Does your name mean something in English?
6. Why does she want to change her name?
7. Why do celebrities use stage names?
8. Is your family name common?

▶ *Listening and Speaking 1, page 18*

B (5 minutes)

1. Direct students to choose five questions from Activity A to ask their partners.

2. Call on volunteers to share information about their partners. Correct use of third-person verbs.

Pronunciation: Intonation in *yes/no* and information questions (5 minutes)

◑ CD1 Tracks 9 and 10

1. Read the information about intonation and play the audio examples.

2. Check comprehension by writing an information question and a *yes/no* question on the board: *What's your name? Is your name Martha?*

3. Ask students whether the questions will be pronounced with rising or falling intonation. Draw the intonation arrows above the questions.

A (5 minutes)
◑ CD1, Track 11

1. Play the audio and ask students to listen and repeat the questions.

2. Call on volunteers to read questions aloud. Provide feedback on intonation.

Activity A Answers, p. 18
1. falling;   **2.** rising;   **3.** falling;   **4.** falling;
5. rising;   **6.** rising;   **7.** falling;   **8.** falling

B (5 minutes)

1. Direct students to read the questions with a partner, focusing on correct intonation.

2. For additional practice, have students turn to Activity A on p. 17 and read the unscrambled questions. Correct intonation if necessary.

 For additional practice with intonation in *yes/no* and information questions, have students visit *Q Online Practice*.

▶ *Listening and Speaking 1, page 19*

Speaking Skill: Asking follow-up questions (5 minutes)

1. Explain the word *follow-up: To follow up means to continue. Follow-up questions are questions that help you continue a conversation.*

2. Read the information about follow-up questions. Have volunteers read the conversation. Point out that the conversation continued because Speaker A asked follow-up questions.

A (10 minutes)

1. Have students look at the pictures of Sanjay and Anita and read the information about them. Check comprehension: *Where is Sanjay from? What kind of music does Anita like? What does Sanjay's name mean?*

2. Have students work with a partner to complete the follow-up questions in the conversation. Go over the answers with the class.

3. Ask partners to read the completed conversation together.

Activity A Answers, pp. 19–20
are you from; big/large; common; mean something; music do you like; your favorite group/band; hobbies

Tip for Success (3 minutes)

1. Direct students to read the tip silently. Provide examples of *yes/no* questions that people might ask when they are getting to know each other.

2. Elicit information questions to replace the *yes/no* questions. Examples: *Do you like to play soccer?* vs. *What sports do you like to play? Are your classes interesting?* vs. *What are you studying?* Point out how much more conversation can be generated with the *Wh-* questions.

B (10 minutes)

1. Have partners work together to write a new conversation between Anita and Sanjay and then take turns reading it aloud.

2. Ask volunteer pairs to read their conversation.

> **Activity B Answers, p. 20**
> Possible conversation:
> **A:** It's nice to meet you, Sanjay. Does your name mean something in English?
> **S:** Yes, it means *winner*.
> **A:** What kind of music do you like?
> **S:** I like alternative rock.
> **A:** What's your favorite band?
> **S:** I really like 80s bands.

MULTILEVEL OPTION

Give lower-level students a frame and ask them to complete the follow-up questions.
A: It's nice to meet you, Sanjay. Where _____ *from?*
S: I'm from _____.
A: Does your name _____?
S: Yes, it means _____.
A: What kind of _____?
S: I like alternative rock.
A: What _____?
S: I like _____.

 For additional practice with asking follow-up questions, have students visit *Q Online Practice*.

▶ *Listening and Speaking 1, page 20*

Unit Assignment: Make an introduction

Unit Question (5 minutes)

Refer students back to the ideas they discussed at the beginning of the unit about whether they like their names. Ask them to look at the notes they took about why they like or don't like their names. Ask if their opinion has changed at all, or if they thought of any new ideas about their names during the course of the unit. Cue students if necessary by asking specific questions about the content of the unit: *We talked about nicknames. Do you like your nickname more or less than your given name? Why did Ringo Starr, Miley Cyrus, and Bruce Lee change their names? Would you change your name? To what?*

Learning Outcome

1. Tie the Unit Assignment to the unit learning outcome. Say: *The outcome for this unit is to interview and introduce a classmate to the class.*

This Unit Assignment is going to let you show your skill at making introductions and speaking in the present tense.

2. Explain that you are going to use a rubric similar to their Self-Assessment checklist on p. 22 to grade their Unit Assignment. Your rubric is slightly different because it is for the students' partner introductions only and not for the partner interviews. Tell students what criteria they will be graded on and how it relates to the criteria in their Self-Assessment checklist.

Consider the Ideas (10 minutes)

1. Direct students to silently read the introduction and check the information that is included.

2. Go over the answers with the class. To help students prepare for the Unit Assignment, discuss alternatives to each piece of information. For example, *Sanjay wrote about what* Anita *means in English. What else could you tell about someone's name?* (the origin of their name, their nickname, how they feel about their name)

> **Consider the Ideas Answers, p. 21**
> Checked: 1, 2, 5, 6, 7

▶ *Listening and Speaking 1, page 21*

Prepare and Speak

Gather Ideas

A (15 minutes)

1. Read the instructions aloud. Seat students in small groups and tell the groups to brainstorm as many questions for each topic as they can before they write down two questions.

2. Demonstrate the procedure by doing a class brainstorm on the first topic, *Name*. Possible questions: *Where does your name come from? What does your name mean in English? Do you have a nickname?* Remind students that *Wh-* questions may get more interesting responses than *yes/no* questions.

Organize Ideas

B (10 minutes)

Tell students to copy the two questions they wrote down for each topic into the chart. Explain that they will use the chart to interview a partner.

Speak

C (20 minutes)

1. Before students conduct their interviews, go over the Self-Assessment checklist on p. 22. Discuss the meaning of each item in the checklist and talk about how to prepare for success with that item. For example, in order to "speak easily," students can practice their introductions ahead of time. To be understood, advise them to speak slowly and at sufficient volume. For present tense, refer students back to the charts on pp. 14–17. For vocabulary, refer them to pp. 5, 9, and 12. For follow-up questions, ask a couple of students to read their chosen questions aloud, and then elicit possible follow-up questions from the class. Briefly review intonation, using questions that students have chosen for their charts.

2. Direct students to interview their partners and write the answers in their chart on p. 21. Tell them to write notes rather than complete sentences. Demonstrate by asking a volunteer a couple of questions and writing short answers on the board.

3. After students have conducted their interview, give them a few minutes to prepare for the introductions by saying it for a new partner or by "thinking it through." Tell them that this is a speaking assignment, and they should not write their introduction out word-for-word.

4. If your class is small, have students use their chart to introduce their partner to the class. Use the Unit Assignment Rubric (on p. 12 of this *Teacher's Handbook*) to score each student's presentation.

5. Alternatively, divide the class into large groups and have students introduce their partners to their group. Have listeners complete the Unit Assignment Rubric.

Alternative Unit Assignments

Assign or have students choose one of these assignments to do instead of, or in addition to, the Unit Assignment:

1. How do people introduce themselves in your country? Do they give their family name first or their given name? Do people usually call each other by their first names? Make a list of advice to give to a visitor to your country about introducing yourself and share it with the class.

2. Work with a partner. Tell your partner a story about you or someone you know who has a nickname. How did you or that person get the nickname?

 For an additional unit assigment, have students visit *Q Online Practice*.

Check and Reflect

Check

A (5 minutes)

1. Direct students to read and complete the Self-Assessment checklist.

2. Ask for a show of hands for how many students gave all or mostly *yes* answers.

3. Congratulate them on their success. Discuss the steps they can take if an item on the checklist was difficult for them. For example, to "speak easily," they need to practice speaking as much as possible. If their partners couldn't understand them, they may need to practice speaking more slowly.

Reflect

B (5 minutes)

1. Refer students to the learning outcome on p. 23. Tell them to talk with their partners about whether they achieved the learning outcome.

2. Have students flip through the unit to discuss the new things they have learned. Then ask them to think about the Unit Question and discuss whether their answer has changed.

Track Your Success (5 minutes)

1. Have students circle the words they have learned in this unit. Suggest that students go back through the unit to review any words they have forgotten.

2. Have students check the skills they have mastered. If students need more practice to feel confident about their proficiency in a skill, point out the page numbers and encourage them to review.

3. Read the learning outcome aloud. Ask students if they feel that they have met the outcome.

Unit Assignment Rubric

Student name: _____

Date: _____

Unit Assignment: *Make an introduction.*

20 points = Introduction element was completely successful (at least 90% of the time).
15 points = Introduction element was mostly successful (at least 70% of the time).
10 points = Introduction element was partially successful (at least 50% of the time).
 0 points = Introduction element was not successful.

Partner Introduction	20 points	15 points	10 points	0 points
Student spoke easily (without long pauses or reading) about a partner's name, background, and interests.				
Student was easy to understand (spoke clearly and at a good speed).				
Student used the simple present tense correctly.				
Student used vocabulary from the unit.				
The introduction included information from follow-up questions.				

Total points: _____

Comments:

Unit QUESTION
How can you find a good job?

Work

LISTENING • listening for key words and phrases
VOCABULARY • using the dictionary
GRAMMAR • simple past
PRONUNCIATION • simple past -*ed* endings
SPEAKING • asking for repetition and clarification

LEARNING OUTCOME

Write interview questions and role-play a job interview.

▶ *Listening and Speaking 1, pages 24-25*
Preview the Unit

Learning Outcome

1. Ask for a volunteer to read the unit skills, then the unit learning outcome.

2. Explain: *This is what you are expected to be able to do by the unit's end. The learning outcome explains how you are going to be evaluated. With this outcome in mind, you should focus on learning these skills (Listening, Vocabulary, Grammar, Pronunciation, Speaking) that will support your goal of writing interview questions and role-playing a job interview. This can also help you act as mentors in the classroom to help the other students meet this outcome.*

A (10 minutes)

1. To help students begin thinking about the topic, write *A Good Job* on the board. Ask students what jobs they think of and what makes the jobs good.

2. Put students in pairs or small groups to discuss the first two questions.

3. Call on volunteers to share their answers with the class. Ask questions: *Is your job a good job? Why or why not? Why is ____ your dream job?*

4. Focus students' attention on the photo. Have a volunteer describe the photo to the class. Read the third question aloud. Discuss where the people are (at a job fair) and what they are doing (meeting potential employers; looking for a job). Ask: *Where else do people look for work?*

Activity A Answers, p. 25
Possible answers:
1. Yes, I have a job; No, but I'm looking for one. I plan to get one in the future.
2. Students may name jobs with high salaries (engineer), jobs with a lot of responsibility (mayor) or flexibility (freelancer), or jobs that reflect a particular interest of theirs (artist).
3. They are at a job fair/recruitment fair. They are looking for a job.

B (15 minutes)

1. Introduce the Unit Question, *How can you find a good job?* Ask related information questions or questions about personal experience to help students prepare for answering the more abstract unit question. *How did you get your last job? Think about some of the dream jobs we just discussed—how can you get those jobs?*

2. Put students in small groups and give each group a piece of poster paper and a marker.

3. Read the Unit Question aloud. Give students a minute to silently consider their answers to the question. Tell students to pass the paper and the marker around the group. Direct each group member to write a different answer to the Unit Question. Encourage them to help one another.

4. Ask each group to choose a reporter to read the answers to the class. Point out similarities and differences among the answers. If answers from different groups are similar, make a class list that incorporates all of the answers. Post the list to refer to later in the unit.

Activity B Answers, p. 25
Possible answers: Lower-level students may answer with single words: *newspaper, friends*. Mid-level students can give more detailed answers: *look on the Internet, look for help-wanted signs in store windows, check classified ads*. Higher-level students may add an evaluative element to their answers: *The best way to get a good job is to get an internship in the field.*

The Q Classroom
CD1, Track 12

1. Play The Q Classroom. Use the examples from the audio to help students continue the conversation. Ask: *How did the students answer the question?* Ask if any ideas from the audio should be added to the lists from Activity B.

2. Ask students to compare the answers from the audio. *Marcus says that the best way to find a good job is through friends. Sophy says that it's important to tell everyone you know that you're looking for work. Felix says that the best way to get a good job is to work your way up. Which way do you think is the best? What experience do you or people you know have with these ways of finding a job?*

▶ *Listening and Speaking 1, page 26*

C (5 minutes)
1. Direct students to match the ads to the photos.
2. Discuss what each person does and what skills they need to have for the job.

Activity C Answers, p. 26
Possible answers:
Website designer: 1, 3; Salesperson: 3, 4;
Server: 3, 4; Teacher: 2, 4

EXPANSION ACTIVITY: Skills and Responsibilities (10 minutes)

To develop students' job-related vocabulary and prepare them for the conversation in Activity D, create a Job Skills/Responsibilities chart on the board. Make two columns with the headings *Skills* and *Responsibilities*. List the four job titles along the side. Elicit skills and responsibilities for each job.

	Skills	Responsibilities
Teacher	good communication; organized	plan classes; teach classes; grade work
Website Designer	computer programming; art & design	work with clients; create designs; program
Server	good with people; good memory	take orders; serve food
Salesperson	persuasive; good communication	sell products; keep track of sales

D (10 minutes)
1. Put students in pairs. Ask them to discuss which jobs they like the best and why.
2. Call on volunteers to tell the class which jobs their partners like best and why.

MULTILEVEL OPTION

Pair students of similar levels. Monitor and assist the lower-level pairs with their conversations. Ask higher-level students to briefly write about their partners' answers when they've finished speaking. When you wrap up the activity, ask lower-level learners to talk about themselves. Ask higher-level learners to talk about their partners.

LISTENING

▶ *Listening and Speaking 1, page 27*

LISTENING 1: Looking for a Job

VOCABULARY (15 minutes)

1. Put students in pairs to read each sentence and write the vocabulary word next to the correct definition.
2. Elicit the answers from volunteers. Then go over each sentence, discussing the vocabulary word. Elicit the part of speech and use the word in a new example or context. For example: *Is career a noun or a verb? What's the difference between a job and a career?*

Group lower-level students and assist them with the task. Provide alternate example sentences to help them understand the words. For example: *I studied for a **career** in teaching. Good computer skills and organization are **requirements** for a secretary. Students take **basic** classes before they take advanced classes. It usually takes four years to earn a college **degree**. When you want a job, you have to complete an **application**.*

Have higher-level students complete the activity individually and then compare answers with a partner. Tell the pairs to write an additional sentence for each word. Have volunteers write one of their sentences on the board. Correct the sentences with the whole class, focusing on the use of the words rather than other grammatical issues.

> **Vocabulary Answers, p. 27**
> **a.** employee; **b.** degree; **c.** career;
> **d.** application; **e.** requirement; **f.** organized;
> **g.** interview; **h.** basic

 For additional practice with the vocabulary, have students visit *Q Online Practice*.

▶ *Listening and Speaking 1, page 28*

PREVIEW LISTENING 1 (3–5 minutes)

1. Direct students to look at the photo. Ask: *Where is she? What do you think she is doing?*

2. Read the introduction and have students check the topics they think the video will include. Tell them they should review their answers after the listening.

> **Preview Listening 1 Answers, p. 28**
> Checked: job requirements; how to get an application

Listening 1 Background Note

Online job recruitment is standard practice these days. Most major companies include information about careers and job openings on their websites. The information can be found under a variety of headings, such as *Jobs at ____, Career Opportunities, Employment Opportunities,* or *Job Listings*. In addition, many employers accept online applications, and prospective employees can post resumes on general job-search sites.

LISTEN FOR MAIN IDEAS (5 minutes)

 CD1, Track 13

1. Direct students to read the sentences before they listen. Play the audio and have students mark the sentences *T* or *F*.

2. Elicit the answers from the class. Elicit a correction for the false sentence.

> **Listen for Main Ideas Answers, p. 28**
> **1.** F; **2.** T; **3.** T; **4.** T; **5.** T

Tip for Success (1 minute)

1. Read the tip aloud.

2. Tell students that they will hear one of these expressions in the audio for the Listen for Details activity.

LISTEN FOR DETAILS (10 minutes)

 CD1, Track 14

1. Direct students to read the statements in the chart before they listen again.

2. As you play the audio, have students listen and check the correct requirement for each job.

3. Have students compare answers with a partner.

4. Replay the audio so that partners can check their answers.

5. Go over the answers with the class.

> **Listen for Details Answers, p. 28**
> Salesperson: students should check 1, 4, 5
> Web Designer: students should check 1, 2, 3, 5

 For additional practice with listening comprehension, have students visit *Q Online Practice*.

▶ *Listening and Speaking 1, page 29*

Critical Thinking Tip (3 minutes)

1. Read the tip aloud.

2. Together, compare two jobs that are similar, such as a doctor and a nurse. Then compare jobs that are less similar, such as a police officer and a construction worker.

WHAT DO YOU THINK? (10 minutes)

1. Ask the students to read the questions and reflect on their answers.

2. Seat students in small groups and assign roles: a group leader to make sure everyone contributes, a note-taker to record the group's ideas, a reporter to share the group's ideas with the class, and a timekeeper to watch the clock.

3. Give students five minutes to discuss the questions. Call time if conversations are winding down. Allow them an extra minute or two if necessary.

4. Call on each group's reporter to share ideas with the class.

What Do You Think? Answers, p. 29
1. must have experience, must be organized;
2. Possible answers: Yes, I meet the requirements for the salesperson job because I'm friendly/organized; No, I don't meet the requirements for the Web designer job because I don't have excellent computer skills.
3. Students may say that a group member with good computer skills is the best person for the Web designer job or that a group member who is very friendly is the best person for the salesperson job.

Critical Q: Expansion Activity

Evaluate Information

Question 3 asks students to determine the best candidate for each job. This engages students in the critical thinking process of evaluation. Help build awareness of this process by having students create a pro and con chart to evaluate a job for themselves. Have them choose one of the jobs and write the positive and negative aspects of the job. See the example chart below.

Salesperson	
+	−
I like working with people. I'm a good self-starter.	I couldn't sell a product I didn't like. Income might be irregular.

Learning Outcome

Use the learning outcome to frame the purpose and relevance of Listening 1. Ask: *What did you learn from Listening 1 that you might use in a job interview?* (Students learned about different job requirements. In an interview, they can explain how their skills meet the requirements of a job.)

Listening Skill: Listening for key words and phrases (5 minutes)

CD1, Track 15

1. Tell students that key words are words that tell the listener what the topic of the conversation is. Play the audio and ask students to put a hand up every time they hear the word *summer* or *job*.

2. Check comprehension by asking questions: *Why should you listen for key words? (They help you identify the topic.) How can you identify the key words? (They are often repeated.)*

A (5 minutes)
CD1, Track 16

1. Play the audio and have students circle the main topic for each section.

2. Ask what the main topics are and allow students to respond orally. Say: *We're going to listen again for the key words and phrases. Then you can check to see if your answers have changed.*

Activity A Answers, p. 29
1. b; 2. a; 3. c; 4. b

▶ *Listening and Speaking 1, page 30*

B (5 minutes)
CD1, Track 17

1. Direct students to listen again and check the words or phrases the speaker uses more than once.

2. Have partners go over Activities A and B and make sure their answers for B fit with their answers for A. Then go over the activities as a class.

Activity B Answers, p. 30
1. growing, success; 2. job; 3. requirements, years of experience; 4. one of our stores, application

 For additional practice with listening for key words and phrases, have students visit *Q Online Practice*.

LISTENING 2: The Right Person for the Job

VOCABULARY (10 minutes)

1. Direct students to read the words and definitions. Pronounce and have students repeat the words.

2. Have students work with a partner to complete the sentences. Call on volunteers to read the completed sentences aloud.

Vocabulary Answers, pp. 30–31
1. major;
2. assistant;
3. advertising;
4. resume;
5. manager;
6. graduate

 For additional practice with the vocabulary, have students visit *Q Online Practice*.

▶ *Listening and Speaking 1, page 31*
PREVIEW LISTENING 2 (3–5 minutes)

1. Read the introduction aloud. Ask students to check which questions they think they will hear.

2. Ask students which questions they did *not* check and why. Tell them they should review their answers after the listening.

Preview Listening 2 Answers, p. 31
Checked: Can you tell me a little about yourself? What was your major in college? Do you have any experience in advertising? Do you have any questions?

Listening 2 Background Note

Additional job interview questions include: *Why did you leave your last job? What do you see yourself doing five years from now? Why did you choose this career? Do you prefer working alone or in teams? What makes you qualified for this position? Why did you decide to seek a position in this company? What two or three things are most important to you in your job? Are you willing to travel?* Students may want to note some of these questions to use in their Unit Assignment role-plays.

Tip for Success (1 minute)

1. Read the tip aloud.

2. Remind students that key words and phrases are often repeated.

LISTEN FOR MAIN IDEAS (5 minutes)

 CD1, Track 18

1. Direct students to look at the chart. Tell them they will check two topics for each person.

2. Play the audio and have students complete the activity individually.

3. Call on a volunteer for the answers.

Listen for Main Ideas Answers, p. 31
Tom: education, skills; Wendy: experience, skills

LISTEN FOR DETAILS (5–10 minutes)

 CD1, Track 19

1. Direct students to read the statements.

2. As you play the audio, have students listen and circle the correct words or phrases.

3. Have students compare answers with a partner.

4. Replay the audio so that the partners can check their answers.

5. Go over the answers with the class.

Listen for Details Answers, pp. 31-32
1. New York; 2. studied; 3. no;
4. convenience store; 5. a little; 6. with others

 For additional practice with listening comprehension, have students visit *Q Online Practice*.

▶ *Listening and Speaking 1, page 32*
WHAT DO YOU THINK?

A (10 minutes)

1. Ask students to read the questions and reflect on their answers.

2. Seat students in small groups and assign roles: a group leader to make sure everyone contributes, a note-taker to record the group's ideas, a reporter to share the group's ideas with the class, and a timekeeper to watch the clock.

3. Give students five minutes to discuss the questions. Call time if conversations are winding down. Allow them an extra minute or two if necessary.

4. Call on each group's reporter to share ideas with the class.

Activity A Answers, p. 32
Possible answers:
1. I think Wendy should get the job because she has experience; I think Tom should get the job because he has art and computer skills.
2. Employers in some countries may ask personal questions such as *Are you married?* and *How old are you?* These questions are not asked in the U.S.

B (5 minutes)

1. Have students continue working in their small groups to discuss the questions in Activity B. Tell them to choose a new leader, note-taker, reporter, and timekeeper.
2. Call on the new reporter to share the group's answers to the questions.

Activity B Answers, p. 32
Possible answers:
1. look for jobs online or at a job fair, complete an application, go to an interview; Yes, the steps are the same in my country.
2. accountant: good at math; carpenter: know how to build things; social worker: have good people skills

Learning Outcome

Use the learning outcome to frame the purpose and relevance of Listenings 1 and 2. Ask: *What did you learn from Listenings 1 and 2 or the Critical Q activity that prepares you for a job interview?* (Students learned about job requirements and how to evaluate job candidates. This will help them determine if a job is right for them.)

Vocabulary Skill: Using the dictionary (3–5 minutes)

1. Direct students to read the information and the dictionary entries.
2. Check comprehension: *What does* career *mean? What does* work *mean?*
3. Elicit examples of jobs that are usually careers (teacher, designer, engineer, health care worker).

Skill Note

Dictionary entries with example sentences can help students make the right word choices. Make a note of words with similar meanings that come up in class and direct students to look in the dictionary to find the difference between them. For additional practice, assign pairs of similar words to groups. Ask the groups to learn the difference in meaning, write

sample sentences, and then share what they learned. Sample pairs include: *shy, quiet; earth, world; fluid, liquid; hear, listen; look, see; ride, drive*

▶ *Listening and Speaking 1, page 33*

A (5 minutes)

1. Have students work with a partner to read the dictionary entries and complete the activity.
2. Go over the answers with the class.

Activity A Answers, p. 33
1. career; **2.** job; **3.** business; **4.** company

B (10 minutes)

1. Direct students to write the sentences.
2. Have students compare sentences with a partner. Then ask volunteers to write their sentences on the board. Correct them together as a class, focusing on the use of the vocabulary.

MULTILEVEL OPTION

Support lower-level students by providing them with additional sentence frames. For *career, job: She has to study hard because she wants a _____ in medicine. He's tired at the end of the day because his _____ is difficult.* For *company, business: He enjoys working for a small _____. They are losing money because they don't understand _____.*

Activity B Answers, p. 33
Possible sentences:
1. I got a job last summer.
2. I think engineering is an interesting career.
3. He works for a large company.
4. The restaurant business can be difficult.

 For additional practice with using a dictionary, have students visit *Q Online Practice*.

▶ *Listening and Speaking 1, page 34*

SPEAKING

Grammar: Simple past (10 minutes)

1. Read the information about forming the simple past with regular verbs. Provide and elicit additional examples for each spelling. For example, most verbs: *talked, called, interviewed;* verbs ending in *e: used, operated, hired;* verbs ending in *y: carried, tried, relied.*

2. Read the information about irregular verbs. Have students repeat the past tense forms. Elicit simple sentences using the verbs.

3. Read the information about negative statements and questions. Point out that the base form of the verb is used with *did* and *didn't*. Elicit additional examples.

Skill Note

Help students memorize the irregular past tense forms by giving "pop quizzes" when you have a few spare moments in class. Say 6–10 verbs in the base form and ask students to write the simple past. Another method is to have students quiz their partners. One partner says the base form, and the other partner says the simple past.

▶ *Listening and Speaking 1, page 35*

A (10 minutes)

1. Direct students to read the conversations and write the correct form of each verb.

2. Ask students to read the completed conversation with a partner, comparing answers as they go.

> **Activity A Answers, p. 35**
> **1.** came; **2.** went; **3.** saw;
> **4.** graduated; **5.** was; **6.** got;
> **7.** took; **8.** wanted; **9.** like;
> **10.** was; **11.** worked; **12.** enjoyed;
> **13.** didn't do; **14.** learned; **15.** study;
> **16.** was; **17.** didn't have

B (5 minutes)

1. Have volunteers read the conversations aloud. Provide feedback on pronunciation.

2. Ask students to practice the conversations with a partner, focusing on correct pronunciation of the past tense verbs.

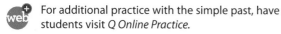 For additional practice with the simple past, have students visit *Q Online Practice*.

▶ *Listening and Speaking 1, page 36*

C (10 minutes)

1. Direct students to read the notes about Carlos. Ask what makes them notes rather than sentences (no subject). Ask: *Why is it important to know how to take notes?* (They allow you to record more information in a shorter period of time.) *When do people take notes?* (at school, when getting information over the telephone, at meetings, when receiving instructions)

2. Ask students to read the questions and write their answers in note form.

D (5 minutes)

Have students ask and answer the questions with a partner. When they finish, have them find a new partner and repeat the activity.

Pronunciation: Simple past *-ed* (5 minutes)

 CD1, Track 20

1. Read the information about the pronunciation of the simple past *–ed* ending. Demonstrate each sound with sample words, e.g., /d/ *studied, rubbed, logged, judged, pulled, hummed, pinned, poured, loved, raised;* /t/ *laughed, liked, skipped, missed, wished, watched;* /əd/ *graded, visited.*

2. Play the audio and have students listen and read along. Say and have students repeat the past tense of each verb.

▶ *Listening and Speaking 1, page 37*

A (5 minutes)

Ask students to take turns saying the simple past forms of the verbs in the box. If they aren't sure, direct them to the explanation on pages 36–37. Show them how to find the final consonant sound and check the corresponding rule.

B (5 minutes)

 CD1, Track 21

1. Direct students to complete the chart.

2. Play the audio and have students check their answers.

> **Activity B Answers, p. 37**
> /t/: liked, looked, washed, stopped
> /d/: changed, required, studied, preferred
> /əd/: completed, needed, wanted, waited

 For additional practice with pronouncing simple past *-ed*, have students visit *Q Online Practice*.

▶ *Listening and Speaking 1, page 38*

C (5 minutes)

1. Read the directions and point out the pronunciation symbol above *completed*. Ask students to underline the regular verbs and write the pronunciation symbols above them.

2. Elicit each verb and write it on the board with the pronunciation symbol. Have students chorally repeat each verb.

> **Activity C Answers, p. 38**
> **1.** /t/: worked, washed; /əd/: wanted, needed;
> **2.** /d/: emailed, joined; /t/: finished; /əd/: completed, printed, graduated, wanted

D (5 minutes)

1. Have students practice the conversations with a partner. Monitor and correct pronunciation of regular past tense verbs.

2. Call on volunteers to read the conversations aloud.

21ST CENTURY SKILLS

Asking for repetition or clarification is a crucial skill for language learners because it has a huge impact on the success of their interactions. Employers are looking for workers who show initiative and take responsibility for their own professional growth, a skill that requires knowing what information you need and how to ask for it.

It's important to provide learners with the language they need to ask for repetition and clarification. Learners also need opportunities to practice in order to really master this important communication skill.

After you have taught the expressions in the Speaking Skill section, encourage students to use them on a regular basis. Make a wall poster with the expressions on it, and whenever a student has a blank look, shakes her head to indicate she doesn't understand, or says *Repeat?* point to the language on the poster and elicit the full request.

Speaking Skill: Asking for repetition and clarification (5 minutes)

Read the information about asking for repetition and have students repeat the phrases.

▶ *Listening and Speaking 1, page 39*

A (5 minutes)
🔊 CD1, Track 22

Play the audio and have students check the phrases they hear.

> **Activity A Answers, p. 39**
> Checked: I didn't catch that; Do you mean…?

B (5 minutes)
🔊 CD1, Track 23

1. Play the audio and direct students to complete the conversations.

2. Have students compare their answers with a partner. Play the audio again so students can check their answers.

3. Go over the answers with the class. Have students chorally repeat the phrases.

> **Activity B Answers, p. 39**
> I'm sorry, I didn't catch that.; I'm sorry. Could you say that again, please?; Could you repeat that?; Do you mean an interview?

Tip for Success (3 minutes)

1. Direct students to read the tip silently.

2. Ask students how they feel about asking people to repeat themselves. Tell them that if they are uncomfortable with it, they should practice frequently in class so that it becomes a habit.

C (5 minutes)

1. Tell students to take turns reading the conversations with a partner.

2. Call on volunteers to read the conversations.

 For additional practice with asking for repetition and clarification, have students visit *Q Online Practice*.

EXPANSION ACTIVITY: Ask for Repetition (10 minutes)

To help students practice using the phrases spontaneously, conduct a mingle activity. Pass out index cards and ask students to write a sentence they might say on the telephone. For example, *Hi, I wanted to talk to you about your interview. Did you get the job at Baxter's? I'd like to talk to Mr. Stevens.* Tell them they are going to mumble the last part of the sentence. Demonstrate with several of their sentences. Have everyone stand and find a partner to say their sentence to (with a mumbled ending). The partner should respond with a request for repetition. After they have clarified each other's sentences, they move on to a new partner. Tell students to use each of the clarification phrases at least once. Participate in the mingle and end the activity when everyone has had a chance to talk to at least four partners.

Learning Outcome

Use the learning outcome to frame the purpose and relevance of the speaking skill. Ask: *Is it a good idea to ask for clarification in a job interview situation? Why?* (Students should note that it's important to ask for clarification in a job interview to make sure they understand the questions correctly.)

▶ *Listening and Speaking 1, page 40*

Ⓠ Unit Assignment: Role-play a job interview

Unit Question (5 minutes)

Refer students back to the ideas they discussed at the beginning of the unit about how to find a good job. Ask them to look at the list they created at that time. Ask if they have gotten any new ideas about the topic during the course of the unit. Cue students if necessary by asking specific questions about the content of the unit: *Some of the job skills we looked at were required for several jobs. What skills were those? We listened to some successful job interviews. What made them successful?*

Learning Outcome

1. Tie the Unit Assignment to the unit learning outcome. Say: *The outcome for this unit is to role-play a job interview. This Unit Assignment is going to let you show your skill at writing interview questions, interviewing, asking for clarification, and speaking in the past tense.*

2. Explain that you are going to use a rubric similar to their Self-Assessment checklist on p. 43 to grade their Unit Assignment. You can also share a copy of the Unit Assignment Rubric (on p. 23 of this *Teacher's Handbook*) with the students.

3. Go over the Self-Assessment checklist on p. 42 in detail. Discuss the meaning of each item in the checklist and talk about how to prepare for success with that item. For example, in order to *speak easily*, tell students to practice interview questions and answers in advance. For *partner understood*, advise them to speak slowly and at sufficient volume. For simple past tense, refer students back to the information on p. 35. For vocabulary, refer them to pp. 27, 31, and 33-34. For asking for clarification, elicit the phrases they practiced from p. 39. Briefly review pronunciation of regular past tense verbs. Write /t/ /d/ and /əd/ on the board and elicit examples of each.

Consider the Ideas

A (10 minutes)

1. Direct students to work with a partner to read the ads and match them to the jobs.

2. Go over the answers with the class.

> **Activity A Answers, p. 40**
> **1.** E; **2.** B; **3.** C; **4.** D; **5.** F; **6.** A

▶ *Listening and Speaking 1, page 41*

B (5 minutes)

1. Have students continue working with their partners to underline the job requirements.

2. Discuss the requirements for each job.

> **Activity B Answers, p. 41**
> **A.** college degree, two years experience;
> **B.** friendly, organized, excellent speaking skills, speak English, French, Spanish;
> **C.** excellent computer skills, online game experience;
> **D.** Experience playing soccer, baseball, basketball, friendly;
> **E.** organized, excellent computer skills, one to two years experience;
> **F.** enjoy working outdoors on big projects

C (10 minutes)

1. Have each pair join another pair to form a small group. Tell them to discuss which jobs they'd like to have and their own qualifications.

2. Call on students from each group to give information about their partners. *Which job did _____ like? Did anyone meet the requirements for the _____ job?*

Prepare and Speak

Gather Ideas

A (10 minutes)

1. Read the directions aloud. Tell students they can use any job that interests them. Emphasize that both partners need to write the requirements for both jobs. Provide questions for guidance: *Does this person need to be friendly? Organized? Creative? Do they need to have computer skills? Communication skills? Technical skills? How much education does this job require? What kind of experience should you have?*

2. Monitor the pairwork and provide feedback.

Organize Ideas

B (10 minutes)

1. Tell students to read the questions and write their answers in their notebooks.

2. While students are writing, walk around and make a note of any common errors you see. Write sentences on the board to represent each error and correct them together. Then ask students to check their own work.

▶ *Listening and Speaking 1, page 42*

Speak

C (15 minutes)

1. If your class is small, have students role-play their job interviews in front of the class.

2. Use the Unit Assignment Rubric (on p. 23) to score each student's role-play.

3. Alternatively, divide the class into large groups and have students do the role-plays for their group. Have listeners complete the Unit Assignment Rubric.

Alternative Unit Assignments

Assign or have students choose one of these assignments to do instead of, or in addition to, the Unit Assignment:

1. What's the best way to get a job? Make a poster of your ideas and present it to your class.

2. You are interested in a job you saw advertised online. With your partner, role-play a phone call to ask for more information.

 For an additional unit assignment, have students visit *Q Online Practice.*

Check and Reflect

Check

A (5 minutes)

1. Direct students to read and complete the Self-Assessment checklist.

2. Ask for a show of hands for how many students gave all or mostly *yes* answers.

3. Congratulate them on their success. Discuss the steps they can take if an item on the checklist was difficult for them. For example, to "speak easily," they need to practice speaking as much as possible. If their partners couldn't understand them, they may need to practice speaking more slowly.

Reflect

 ### B (5 minutes)

1. Refer students to the learning outcome on p. 43. Tell them to talk with their partners about whether they achieved the learning outcome. They may also want to flip through the unit to discuss the new things they learned.

2. Then ask them to think about the Unit Question and discuss any new answers they have for the question.

▶ *Listening and Speaking 1, page 43*

Track Your Success (5 minutes)

1. Have students circle the words they learned in this unit. Suggest that they go back through the unit to review any words they have forgotten.

2. Have students check the skills they have mastered. If students need more practice to feel confident about their proficiency in a skill, point out the page numbers and encourage them to review.

3. Read the learning outcome aloud. Ask students if they feel that they have met the outcome.

Unit Assignment Rubric

Student name: _____

Date: _____

Unit Assignment: *Role-play a job interview.*

20 points = Interview element was completely successful (at least 90% of the time).
15 points = Interview element was mostly successful (at least 70% of the time).
10 points = Interview element was partially successful (at least 50% of the time).
 0 points = Interview element was not successful.

Interview Role-play	20 points	15 points	10 points	0 points
Student answered job interview questions easily (without long pauses or reading) and was easy to understand (spoke clearly and at a good speed).				
Student used the simple past tense correctly.				
Student used vocabulary from the unit.				
Student asked for clarification appropriately.				
Student pronounced the past tense of regular verbs correctly.				

Total points: _____

Comments

Unit QUESTION:

Why do we study other cultures?

Long Distance

LISTENING • taking notes in a T-chart
VOCABULARY • guessing words in context
GRAMMAR • *should* and *shouldn't* and *it's* + (*not*) adjective + infinitive
PRONUNCIATION • the schwa /ə/ sound
SPEAKING • presenting information from notes

LEARNING OUTCOME

Give a presentation about customs in a culture you know well.

▶ *Listening and Speaking 1, pages 44–45*

Preview the Unit

Learning Outcome

1. Ask for a volunteer to read the unit skills, then the unit learning outcome.

2. Explain: *This is what you are expected to be able to do by the unit's end. The learning outcome explains how you are going to be evaluated. With this outcome in mind, you should focus on learning these skills (Listening, Vocabulary, Grammar, Pronunciation, Speaking) that will support your goal of giving a presentation about cultural customs. This can also help you act as mentors in the classroom to help the other students meet this outcome.*

A (10 minutes)

1. Prepare students for the topic by telling them a little bit about yourself, about time you have spent in another country, and some interesting things about the culture there. If your culture is different from your students', share a couple of well-known aspects about it as well.

2. Put students in pairs or small groups to discuss the first two questions.

3. Call on volunteers to share their ideas with the class. Ask questions: *Is it interesting to learn about other cultures? Do you think it's important to learn about other cultures? What's a good way to learn about other cultures if you can't travel?*

4. Focus students' attention on the photo. Have a volunteer describe the photo to the class. Ask: *Where do you think these people are from? Are any of them from the same country?* Read the third question aloud. Elicit answers from volunteers.

Activity A Answers, p. 45
Possible answers:
1. Yes, I went to Mexico on vacation; No, but I really want to go to Japan.
2. Students may mention food, language, sports, landmarks, history, current events, music, etc.
3. They may be talking about what they are wearing, why they wear it, and when they wear it. They may be talking about where they are from.

B (15 minutes)

1. Introduce the Unit Question, *Why do we study other cultures?* Ask related information questions or questions about personal experience to help students prepare for answering the more abstract unit question. *Have you studied other cultures in school or watched documentaries about other cultures? What did you learn that was interesting?*

2. Tell the students, *Let's start off our discussion by listing things that are sometimes different in different cultures. We could start our list with food because people from different cultures eat different foods. But there are many more cultural differences than what we eat. What else can be different?*

3. Seat students in small groups and direct them to pass around a paper as quickly as they can, with each group member adding one item to the list. Tell them they have two minutes to make the lists and they should write as much as possible.

4. Call time and ask a reporter from each group to read the list aloud.

5. Use items from the list as a springboard for discussion. For example, *From our lists, we see that people from different cultures may dress differently, listen to different music, have different customs, etc. Why should we learn about these things?*

Activity B Answers, p. 45
Possible answers: Lower-level students may give a short answer: *It's interesting to learn about people.* Mid-level students can briefly expand: *We need to study other cultures so that we can do business and get along with all kinds of people.* Higher-level students might explain in more depth: *The world is getting smaller, so it's important that different cultures learn about each other so they can improve relations and promote peace.*

The Q Classroom

CD1, Track 24

1. Play The Q Classroom. Use the example from the audio to help students continue the conversation. Ask: *How did the students answer the question? Do you agree or disagree with their ideas? Why?*

2. Say: *On the audio, Sophy says that when we study other cultures, we learn about how we are the same. Let's discuss this idea.* Elicit things that different cultures have in common (love of family, desire for a good life, appreciation for art and music, etc.)

▶ *Listening and Speaking 1, page 46*

C (10 minutes)

1. Direct students to look at the graphic organizer and read the instructions. Elicit an example for each of the categories. Encourage students to name and describe each item, e.g., *Capoeira is a Brazilian martial art done to music.*

MULTILEVEL OPTION

Allow lower-level students to put words in their own language in the chart, e.g., *salsa or kimchee.* Encourage higher-level students to describe the item rather than just name it: *dancing music called salsa; a spicy cabbage dish called kimchee.*

For Activity D, use mixed-level groups and ask higher-level students to help the others explain the items in their chart.

D (10 minutes)

1. Seat students in groups and have them share one item from their chart. Ask groups who finish early to share more items.

2. If your students are from different cultures, call on individuals to share something they learned about someone else's culture. If they are from the same culture, ask them to share items from different parts of the chart.

EXPANSION ACTIVITY: Culture Walk-Around
(10 minutes)

1. To give students a little more practice talking about culture, conduct a question-and-answer walk-around. Write a list of items on the board that students mentioned during Activities C and D. Be sure that you have at least one item to represent every culture in the room. If your students are all from the same culture, make a list of items from other cultures you think at least one student may be familiar with, e.g., *taco, pizza, karate, kung fu, sari, kimono, Bonjour, polka, etc.*

2. Direct students to walk around the room, find a partner, and ask *Excuse me, what is _____?* (a word from the board). Partners should ask and answer one question each and then move on to a new partner. Put a sentence frame on the board to help them answer the question. *Capoeira is a martial art from Brazil.*

LISTENING

▶ *Listening and Speaking 1, page 47*

LISTENING 1: International Advertising

VOCABULARY (15 minutes)

1. Direct students to read the conversations and match the definitions to the bold words.

2. Have partners compare answers. Elicit the answers from volunteers. Have students repeat the vocabulary words.

3. Ask questions to help students connect with the vocabulary: *Name an **international** company. What do you have **difficulty** understanding in English class? What is something you often **avoid** doing?*

4. Ask the partners to read the conversations.

Vocabulary Answers, p. 47
1. f; **2.** b; **3.** d; **4.** h; **5.** a; **6.** e; **7.** c; **8.** g

 For additional practice with the vocabulary, have students visit *Q Online Practice*.

Tip for Success (2 minutes)

1. Read the tip aloud.
2. Discuss how study groups can help students better understand what they are learning.

▶ *Listening and Speaking 1, page 48*

PREVIEW LISTENING 1 (5 minutes)

1. Direct students to look at the photo. Ask: *What is this a picture of? What do you think its cultural meaning is?* (The photo is of a maneki neko. It is a Japanese ceramic sculpture that is found in many shops in Asia.)

2. Read the introductory paragraph and the answer choices aloud. Have students check their answers. Tell students they should review their answers after the listening.

Preview Listening 1 Answers, p. 48
Checked: language mistakes; problems with colors; problems with different customs

Listening 1 Background Note

Different numbers in different cultures have significance. Many hotels in English-speaking countries do not have a room 13 or a 13th floor, and in Japan, the numbers 4 and 9 are sometimes avoided. Some Chinese numbers are considered to be positive or negative based on words with similar pronunciations. Because there are a variety of dialects of Chinese, a number may be considered positive in one area and negative in another, although 4 is generally considered negative and 8 positive. Advertisers sometimes avoid using particular numbers, even in advertised prices.

LISTEN FOR MAIN IDEAS (5 minutes)

 CD1, Track 25

1. Ask students to read the statements. Have them predict which ideas they will hear.
2. Play the audio and have students complete the activity individually.
3. Elicit the answers from the class.

Listen for Main Ideas Answers, p. 48
Checked: a; c; e

LISTEN FOR DETAILS (10 minutes)

 CD1, Track 26

1. Direct students to read the chart.
2. As you play the audio, have students listen and check the correct items in the chart.
3. Have students compare answers with a partner.
4. Replay the audio so that the partners can check their answers.
5. Go over the answers with the class.

Listen for Details Answers, p. 48
Example 1: a computer company; Eastern Europe; the product name means *chicken*. Example 2: a telephone company; the Middle East; the advertisement showed the bottom of a man's shoes.

 For additional practice with listening comprehension, have students visit *Q Online Practice*.

▶ *Listening and Speaking 1, page 49*

WHAT DO YOU THINK? (10 minutes)

1. Ask students to read the questions and reflect on their answers.
2. Seat students in small groups and assign roles: a group leader to make sure everyone contributes, a note-taker to record the group's ideas, a reporter to share the group's ideas with the class, and a timekeeper to watch the clock.
3. Give students five minutes to discuss the questions. Call time if conversations are winding down. Allow them an extra minute or two if necessary.

4. Call on each group's reporter to share ideas with the class.

What Do You Think? Answers, p. 49
Possible answers:
1. Companies need to think about the language and customs of the culture where they are advertising. Students may know the names of foreign products which are amusing in their language.
2. Students may talk about colors that hold patriotic significance or that are used in traditional ceremonies, like weddings or funerals.

Learning Outcome

Use the learning outcome to frame the purpose and relevance of Listening 1. Ask: *What did you learn from Listening 1 that prepares you to give a presentation about a culture?* (Students learned about mistakes people/companies can make in other cultures.)

Listening Skill: Taking notes in a T-chart (5 minutes)

1. Draw a large capital *T* on the board and ask: *What letter is this?* Explain to students that they are going to learn about taking notes in a T-chart. Ask students to read the introductory information.

2. Check comprehension by asking questions: *What do you write on the left side of the chart? What do you write on the right? What are details?*

Tip for Success (1 minute)

1. Read the tip aloud.
2. Remind students that key words are often repeated and can help them identify the main idea or topic.

▶ *Listening and Speaking 1, page 50*

A (5 minutes)
 CD1, Track 27

1. Direct students to look over the chart.
2. Play the audio and ask students to complete the chart. Elicit the answers from the class.

Activity A Answers, p. 50
1. It's important for companies to know the meaning of colors in different cultures.
2. good luck;
3. blue;
4. white;
5. White

B (5 minutes)
 CD1, Track 28

1. Play the next part of the audio and have students take notes in the chart. Remind them to put the main idea on the left and the details on the right.

2. Have students compare their answers with a partner. Elicit answers from volunteers and complete the chart on the board.

Activity B Answers, p. 50

Main Ideas	Details
International companies should learn about numbers in different cultures.	-Some numbers can be good in one culture and bad in another. -Example: Sports company in Korea wanted to sell golf balls, but put four balls in each package. In Korea, the number four sounds like the word for *death*.

 For additional practice with taking notes in a T-chart, have students visit *Q Online Practice*.

▶ *Listening and Speaking 1, page 51*

LISTENING 2: Cultural Problems

VOCABULARY (10 minutes)

1. Direct students to read the words and definitions in the box. Pronounce and have students repeat the words.

2. Have students work with a partner to complete the sentences. Call on volunteers to read the completed sentences aloud.

3. Have the pairs read the sentences together.

Vocabulary Answers, p. 51
1. invite; 2. upset; 3. rude; 4. offended;
5. dies; 6. wedding; 7. confused; 8. carefully

For additional practice with the vocabulary, have students visit *Q Online Practice*.

▶ *Listening and Speaking 1, page 52*

PREVIEW LISTENING 2 (5 minutes)

1. Direct students' attention to the photos and ask: *Where are the people? What are they doing?*

2. Elicit the students' ideas about what cultural problems the photos show. Write their ideas on the board for review after the listening.

Listening 2 Background Note

The distance people like to keep between themselves and others is sometimes called "personal space." Personal space preferences vary from culture to culture. They also vary with gender, relationship, situation, and individual preference.

Most cultures have many customs associated with gift-giving—when to give or open gifts and what is appropriate to give a dinner host, a co-worker, or a teacher are interesting topics of discussion if you have students from a variety of cultures.

All people doing international business need to be aware that business card etiquette varies from culture to culture. The rules of etiquette dictate when to give cards, to whom to give them, what their content should be, and how to treat the cards you receive.

LISTEN FOR MAIN IDEAS (5 minutes)

CD1, Track 29

1. Direct students to read the answer choices. Tell them they will check one main idea for each story.
2. Play the audio and have students complete the activity individually.
3. Call on a volunteer for the answers.

> **Listen for Main Ideas Answers, p. 52**
> **1.** b; **2.** c; **3.** a

LISTEN FOR DETAILS (5 minutes)

CD1, Track 30

1. Direct students to read the statements before they listen again.
2. As you play the audio, have students listen and mark the sentences *T* or *F*.
3. Have students compare answers with a partner.
4. Replay the audio so that the partners can check their answers.
5. Go over the answers with the class. Elicit corrections for the false statements.

> **Listen for Details Answers, p. 52**
> **1.** F; **2.** F; **3.** T; **4.** F; **5.** T; **6.** T

 For additional practice with listening comprehension, have students visit *Q Online Practice*.

▶ *Listening and Speaking 1, page 53*

WHAT DO YOU THINK?

A (10 minutes)

1. Ask students to read the questions and reflect on their answers.
2. Seat students in small groups and assign roles: a group leader to make sure everyone contributes, a note-taker to record the group's ideas, a reporter to share the group's ideas with the class, and a timekeeper to watch the clock.
3. Give students five minutes to discuss the questions. Call time if conversations are winding down. Allow them an extra minute or two if necessary.
4. Call on each group's reporter to share ideas with the class.

> **Activity A Answers, p. 53**
> **1.** Yes, I do; No, I don't.
> **2.** In addition to the kinds of problems mentioned in the lesson, students may be able to share problems or situations that they or someone they know has experienced because of cultural differences.

B (5 minutes)

1. Have students continue working in their small groups to discuss the questions in Activity B. Tell them to choose a new leader, note-taker, reporter, and timekeeper.
2. Call on the new reporter to share the group's answers to the questions.

> **Activity B Answers, p. 53**
> Possible answers:
> **1.** People may accidentally cause offense; they may get the wrong impression; they may get angry; they may lose business or friendship opportunities.
> **2.** They should know that it's OK to arrive a little late to social gatherings; that we divide a restaurant bill evenly among the diners regardless of what they ordered; that you should never write a person's name in red ink.

Learning Outcome

Use the learning outcome to frame the purpose and relevance of Listenings 1 and 2. Ask: *What did you learn from Listenings 1 and 2 that will help you give a presentation about a culture? What topics might you want to talk about?* (Students learned about different customs in different countries and mistakes people can make. In their presentations, they may want to talk about appropriate behavior in different situations.)

Vocabulary Skill: Words in context
(5 minutes)

1. Direct students to read the information silently.

2. Check comprehension: *What is context? How can it help you? What helps you understand the meaning of* confused *in the example?*

Skill Note

Point out to students that it's important for comprehension that they try to figure out the meaning of words from context rather than stopping and looking up words in their dictionary. Reinforce this in class. When students ask what a word means, review the context clues around the word and encourage them to guess, at least approximately, what the word means. (You may want to teach them the precise definition after they've made their guess.)

▶ *Listening and Speaking 1, page 54*

A (5 minutes)
CD1, Track 31

1. Tell students not to use their dictionaries for this exercise. Play the audio and ask them to circle the meaning of each word.

2. Go over the answers with the class.

> **Activity A Answers, p. 54**
> **1.** a; **2.** b; **3.** a; **4.** b; **5.** a

B (10 minutes)
CD1, Track 32

1. Play number 1 and point out how the words *first time away*, and *missed my family* provide a clue that the word *depressed* has something to do with sadness. Tell students to listen to the rest of the audio and write the context clues they hear.

2. Have partners compare answers. Play the audio again so they can check their answers together. Go over the answers as a class.

> **Activity B Answers, p. 54**
> **2.** lonely, wanted to go home;
> **3.** great, kind;
> **4.** like a member of the family;
> **5.** didn't miss home, happy, didn't want to come home

 For additional practice with guessing the meaning of words in context, have students visit *Q Online Practice*.

▶ *Listening and Speaking 1, page 55*

SPEAKING

Grammar Part 1: *Should* and *shouldn't*
(5 minutes)

1. Read the information about using *should* and *shouldn't*. Provide and elicit additional examples: *In the U.S., you shouldn't ask people how much money they make. You shouldn't ask adults how old they are. When you meet someone, you should shake hands firmly. Visitors should tip service people.*

2. Check comprehension by asking questions: *What form of the verb do we use after* should *or* shouldn't? *What does* should *mean? What does* shouldn't *mean?* Point out that *should* and *shouldn't* don't change if the subject changes.

Skill Note

Modals like *should* can be confusing for students because they don't exist in many languages. Students can get used to using *should* and *shouldn't* with the context that is familiar to them all—the classroom. Seat them in small groups and ask each group to come up with a list of *shoulds* and *shouldn'ts* for English class. Elicit items from the lists and see if everyone agrees on appropriate English-class behavior.

A (10 minutes)
CD1, Track 33

1. Direct students to work with a partner to circle *should* or *shouldn't*. Encourage them to ask other students if they don't know the answer.

2. Play the audio. Have the partners correct their answers and then read the sentences together.

Activity A Answers, p. 55
1. shouldn't; **2.** shouldn't; **3.** should;
4. should; **5.** shouldn't; **6.** should

▶ *Listening and Speaking 1, page 56*

B (10 minutes)

1. Direct students to work individually to write
   the sentences.

2. Have them read their sentences with a partner.
   Ask volunteers to write sentences on the board.

3. If your students are from different cultures, ask
   how many of them have the same or similar
   customs as the ones on the board. Leave these
   sentences on the board for the next activity.

Activity B Answers, p. 56
Possible answers: You should bow when you are
formally introduced to someone. You shouldn't eat
while you're walking.

 For additional practice with *should* and *shouldn't*,
have students visit *Q Online Practice*.

Grammar Part 2: *It's* + adjective
+ infinitive (5 minutes)

1. Read the information and the example sentences.
   Ask students to identify each infinitive verb.

2. Check comprehension. Ask students to look at the
   should sentences on the board from the previous
   activity and lead them through the process of
   converting them into *it's* + *(not)* adjective +
   infinitive sentences. For example: *You shouldn't ask
   people about their salaries* becomes *It's not polite to
   ask people about their salaries.*

A (5 minutes)

🔊 CD1, Track 34

1. Play the audio and have students complete the
   missing information.

2. Ask volunteers to write the sentences on
   the board.

Activity A Answers, p. 56
1. It's rude to stand too close.
2. It's OK to give an odd number.
3. It's not polite to do that.

▶ *Listening and Speaking 1, page 57*

B (10 minutes)

1. Read the directions aloud and elicit a couple of
   examples from volunteers. Have students work
   individually to write their sentences.

2. While students are writing, monitor and provide
   assistance as needed.

Activity B Answers, p. 57
Possible answers: It's polite to take off your shoes in the
house. It's rude to show the bottoms of your feet.

MULTILEVEL OPTION

Seat students in mixed-ability pairs. Direct them
to come up with the sentences orally before writing
them down. Ask the higher-level students to assist
their lower-level classmates with spelling and
grammar.

C (10 minutes)

1. Seat students in small groups. Ask them to take
   turns reading one sentence at a time. Encourage
   group members to comment and ask follow-up
   questions. Write phrases and sentence frames on
   the board to help them with this: *That's interesting!
   I didn't know that. That's also true in _____ culture.*

2. As a follow-up, call on individuals to share
   the most interesting sentence they heard in
   their group.

Pronunciation: The schwa /ə/ sound
(5 minutes)

🔊 CD1, Track 35

1. Read the information about the schwa. Write the
   example words on the board and underline the
   stressed syllable to demonstrate visually how the
   unstressed syllable has the schwa sound.

2. Check comprehension. Write *offend* and *product*
   on the board and elicit the stressed syllable
   (off<u>end</u>; <u>prod</u>uct). Point out that the other vowel is
   pronounced with the schwa sound.

Skill Note

The schwa is a useful way of demonstrating to students how crucial word stress is to the pronunciation of English. Whenever you teach a multi-syllable word, ask students to identify the stressed syllable and point out vowels that are reduced to schwa. Also point out the role of schwa in sentence stress. For example, *to* and *do* are pronounced with a long *u* out of context, but in a sentence, they are normally unstressed and pronounced with the schwa sound.

The sound /ʌ/ (as in the first syllable of *custom*) is slightly longer than the schwa, but at normal conversational speeds is often pronounced the same way.

A (5 minutes)

CD1, Track 36

1. Have students listen and underline the schwa sound in each word.

2. Elicit answers from volunteers. If there are any difficulties, elicit the stressed syllable of the word and point out that schwa falls elsewhere.

> **Activity A Answers, p. 57**
> **1.** avoid;   **2.** bottom;   **3.** considerate;
> **4.** mistake;   **5.** personality;   **6.** positive;
> **7.** similar;   **8.** telephone

▶ *Listening and Speaking 1, page 58*

B (10 minutes)

1. Have students work individually to write sentences.

2. Pair students and have them read their sentences aloud. Monitor and provide feedback on pronunciation.

 For additional practice with the schwa sound, have students visit *Q Online Practice*.

Speaking Skill: Presenting information from notes (5 minutes)

1. Direct students to read the information about speaking from notes.

2. Check comprehension: *Why should you make eye contact with the audience? How should you prepare? Why is it important to use small cards? To write only key words? To practice? What should you do while you're speaking?*

Speaking from notes is something students may need to do in their professional lives as well as in their academic lives, but it can be nerve-wracking and difficult. Help them become comfortable with this important skill through extensive practice. Conduct short speech activities as you work through each unit. (This will usually help them prepare for the Unit Assignment as well.) Assign a very specific topic, for example, in this unit, *gift-giving in my culture*. Pass out small notecards and direct students to plan a 30-second speech on the topic, writing no more than five or six words on the card. Then put the students in groups and have them deliver their mini-speeches to the group.

▶ *Listening and Speaking 1, page 59*

A (10 minutes)

1. Direct students to look at the Web page. Remind students that key words and phrases are often repeated. Have them work individually to complete the activity.

2. Elicit the answers from the class orally.

> **Activity A Answers, p. 59**
> Possible answers: Eating: only right hand, impolite left hand; offer more food, should take more; Visiting: dress neatly and conservatively; bring chocolates/sweets, isn't good to bring flowers; Gift-giving: receive a gift with right hand, shouldn't use left hand; shouldn't open, wait until later.

▶ *Listening and Speaking 1, page 60*

B (10 minutes)

1. Tell students to look at the phrases they underlined and use them to complete the outline.

2. Call on volunteers to read the completed items aloud. Provide feedback on pronunciation.

> **Activity B Answers, p. 60**
> **1.** your left hand; offer more food; take more;
> **2.** Visiting; dress neatly; a gift; chocolates or sweets; flowers;
> **3.** Gift-giving; with your right hand; your left hand; open it later

Tip for Success (1 minute)

1. Read the tip aloud.
2. Point out that even though they should practice their presentation, they shouldn't try to memorize it word-for-word.

C (10 minutes)

1. Pair students and have them practice presenting the information to a partner.
2. Monitor and provide feedback on eye contact. If students are reading too much, have them switch partners and practice again.

 For additional practice with presenting information from notes, have students visit *Q Online Practice*.

Q Unit Assignment: Give a presentation

Unit Question (5 minutes)

Refer students back to the ideas they discussed at the beginning of the unit about why people study other cultures. Cue students if necessary by asking specific questions about the content of the unit: *What kinds of cultural differences did we talk about? What differences did we see that might cause misunderstandings?*

Learning Outcome

1. Tie the Unit Assignment to the unit learning outcome. Say: *The outcome for this unit is to give a presentation about a culture you know well. This Unit Assignment is going to let you show your skill in using* should/shouldn't *and it's + adjective + infinitive, pronouncing the schwa, and presenting information from notes.*
2. Explain that you are going to use a rubric similar to their Self-Assessment checklist on p. 62 to grade their Unit Assignment. You can also share a copy of the Unit Assignment Rubric (on p. 34 of this *Teacher's Handbook*) with the students.

▶ *Listening and Speaking 1, page 61*

Consider the Ideas (10 minutes)

1. Direct students to look again at the Web page on p. 59. Elicit some of the information they learned about Egypt. Seat them in small groups and ask them to discuss the questions.
2. Call on volunteers to share the ideas they talked about in their groups.

Consider the Ideas Answers, p. 61

Possible answers:
1. Yes. In my culture it's polite to bring sweets when you visit someone.
2. Yes, because you might offend people in your host country. You'll get more out of your visit, and you're more likely to make friends with people in the host country; No, because if you're visiting, you may just be looking at the sights, and learning the customs may not be necessary.

Prepare and Speak

Gather Ideas

A (10 minutes)

1. Direct students to choose three topics from the box and write them in the chart. Point out that on the right side of the chart, they should write notes, not complete sentences. Demonstrate on the board by writing a complete sentence: *In the United States, when you visit someone's house, you should come on time.* Elicit how much of the sentence would be written in the chart (*come on time*).
2. While students are working, monitor and provide feedback on their note-taking.

▶ *Listening and Speaking 1, page 62*

Critical Q: Expansion Activity

Apply Knowledge

Point out to students that applying their knowledge to do something new is what helps them take possession of what they've learned. Take it a step further by having them apply the knowledge they learn from their classmates' presentations by making a comparison chart.

Direct students to take notes while their classmates are presenting. Then have each student create a comparison chart by labeling columns with topics they heard about in several different presentations, e.g., color, manners, symbols, etc., and writing what they learned about different cultures in each column.

Critical Thinking Tip (1 minute)

1. Read the tip aloud.
2. Remind students that preparing a presentation ensures that they will present their ideas in a clear way.

Organize Ideas

B (10 minutes)

1. Have students transfer the notes from their charts onto notecards.

2. Remind students that practice is an important part of preparation. Have them practice their presentations with a partner.

Speak

C (10-15 minutes)

1. Remind students to review the Self-Assessment checklist on p. 62 before they give their presentations. Call on students to give their presentations to the class.

2. Use the Unit Assignment Rubric on p. 34 of this *Teacher's Handbook* to score each student's presentation.

3. Alternatively, divide the class into large groups and have students give their presentations to their group. Have listeners complete the Unit Assignment Rubric.

Alternative Unit Assignments

Assign or have students choose one of these assignments to do instead of, or in addition to, the Unit Assignment.

1. Imagine that you work for the advertising department of an international company. Think of a product and decide where you will sell it. Make an advertisement for the product. Think about the customs of that country.

2. Tell about a cultural problem you had when you visited another culture or when you met a person from another culture. Make notes and give a presentation to your classmates.

 For an additional unit assignment, have students visit *Q Online Practice*.

Check and Reflect

Check

A (5 minutes)

1. Direct students to read and complete the Self-Assessment checklist.

2. Ask for a show of hands for how many students gave all or mostly *yes* answers.

3. Congratulate them on their success. Discuss the steps they can take if an item on the checklist was difficult for them. For example, if they had trouble speaking from notes, they should practice this skill whenever they get a chance, writing key words on notecards and speaking without memorizing.

Reflect

 B (5 minutes)

1. Refer students to the learning outcome on p. 63. Tell them to talk with their partners about whether they achieved the learning outcome.

2. Elicit the answers to the Unit Question that students came up with at the beginning of the unit. Encourage them to flip through the unit as they discuss the new things they learned and new answers they may have to the Unit Question.

▶ *Listening and Speaking 1, page 63*

Track Your Success (5 minutes)

1. Have students circle the words they have learned in this unit. Suggest that students go back through the unit to review any words they have forgotten.

2. Have students check the skills they have mastered. If students need more practice to feel confident about their proficiency in a skill, point out the page numbers and encourage them to review.

3. Read the learning outcome aloud. Ask students if they feel that they have met the outcome.

Unit 3　Long Distance

Unit Assignment Rubric

Student name: _____

Date: _____

Unit Assignment: *Give a presentation.*

20 points = Presentation element was completely successful (at least 90% of the time).
15 points = Presentation element was mostly successful (at least 70% of the time).
10 points = Presentation element was partially successful (at least 50% of the time).
　0 points = Presentation element was not successful.

Give a Presentation	20 points	15 points	10 points	0 points
Student spoke easily about cultural customs (without long pauses or reading) and was easy to understand (spoke clearly and at a good speed).				
Student used *should/should not* and *it's* + (*not*) adjective + infinitive correctly.				
Student used vocabulary from the unit.				
Student presented information from notes.				
Student correctly pronounced any words with schwa.				

Total points: _____

Comments:

Unit QUESTION

What makes a happy ending?

Positive Thinking

LISTENING • using information questions to understand a story
VOCABULARY • using the dictionary
GRAMMAR • *because* and *so*
PRONUNCIATION • syllables and syllable stress
SPEAKING • responding in a conversation

LEARNING OUTCOME

Participate in a group discussion about bad situations with happy endings.

Listening and Speaking 1, page 64-65

Preview the Unit

Learning Outcome

1. Ask for a volunteer to read the unit skills, then the unit learning outcome.

2. Explain: *This is what you are expected to be able to do by the unit's end. The learning outcome explains how you are going to be evaluated. With this outcome in mind, you should focus on learning these skills (Listening, Vocabulary, Grammar, Pronunciation, Speaking) that will support your goal of participating in a group discussion about bad situations with happy endings. This can also help you act as mentors in the classroom to help the other students meet this outcome.*

A (10 minutes)

1. Prepare students for thinking about the topic by asking questions about happy endings: *What are some famous stories with happy endings? What happens?*

2. Put students in pairs or small groups to discuss the first two questions.

3. Call on volunteers to share their ideas with the class. Ask additional questions: *Why are happy endings popular? What is your favorite happy ending from a movie or story?*

4. Focus students' attention on the photo. Have a volunteer describe the photo to the class. Ask: *What happened to the tree? What happened to the car? How would you feel if this were your car?* Read the third question aloud. Elicit answers from volunteers.

Activity A Answers, p. 65
Possible answers:
1. Yes, because they make me feel good; No, because sometimes they aren't realistic.
2. Yes, you can learn from a bad situation or some unexpected good can come from a bad situation.
3. The photo shows a happy ending for the owner of the car because it wasn't damaged. It doesn't show a happy ending for the owner of the car if he/she has to get somewhere important and the car is blocked by the tree.

B (15 minutes)

1. Introduce the Unit Question, *What makes a happy ending?* Ask related information questions or questions about personal experience to help students prepare for answering the more abstract unit question. *What is something that happened to you that had a happy ending? Have you ever been in a bad situation that had a happy ending?*

2. Put students in small groups and give each group a piece of poster paper and a marker.

3. Read the Unit Question aloud. Give students a minute to silently consider their answers to the question. Tell students to pass the paper and the marker around the group. Direct each group member to write a different answer to the question. Encourage them to help one another.

4. Ask each group to choose a reporter to read the answers to the class. Point out similarities and differences among the groups' answers. If answers from different groups are similar, make a group list that incorporates all of the answers. Post the list for students to refer to later in the unit.

5. Ask students to sit down, copy the Unit Question, and make a note of their answers. They will refer back to these notes at the end of the unit.

Activity B Answers, p. 65

Possible answers: Lower-level students may give one-word answers: *success*. Mid-level students can expand with a brief explanation: *A happy ending is when something good happens to someone, like finding success or true love*. Higher-level students can expand on their opinions: *Sometimes bad things happen that make us unhappy. We can't control random events that happen. But good things can often come from a bad situation*.

The Q Classroom

CD1, Track 37

1. Play The Q Classroom. Use the example from the audio to help students continue the conversation.

2. Ask: *How did the students answer the question? Do you agree or disagree with their ideas? Why?*

3. Marcus says, "Sometimes a happy ending can come from something bad." Ask students if they agree with Marcus and why or why not.

▶ *Listening and Speaking 1, page 66*

C (10 minutes)

Direct students to look at the chart and write their answers with their partner. Discuss their answers as a class.

> **Activity C Answers, p. 66**
> Students may provide happy endings from traditional stories or contemporary movies or books. Some examples: Snow White (She's woken by the prince.); Finding Nemo (Nemo's father finds him.); and Wall-E (Earth gets re-populated.).

D (10 minutes)

Have students read the situations in the chart and check the ending they think each situation would have.

> **Activity D Answers, p. 66**
> Answers will vary.

E (10 minutes)

1. Seat students in groups and direct them to discuss what they think might happen next in each situation from Activity D.

2. Elicit ideas from around the room. Continue until the students have no more ideas.

EXPANSION ACTIVITY: Add details (10 minutes)

1. Seat students in groups. Give each group a sheet of poster paper and tell them to take turns writing their "possible endings" for the situations in Activity D. For example, if they checked *Happy* for number 1, they could write: *Paul did well on the test because he knew all of the information*.

2. Have each group share its poster with the class. Discuss which endings seem the most likely and why.

LISTENING

▶ *Listening and Speaking 1, page 67*

LISTENING 1: A Bad Situation with a Happy Ending

Tip for Success (1 minute)

1. Read the tip after students have completed the vocabulary activity on page 67.

2. Ask students to identify the context clues in the first sentence (*hikers, for the night*).

3. Repeat the process with the other sentences.

VOCABULARY (10 minutes)

1. Direct students to read the words and definitions in the box. Pronounce and have students repeat the words.

2. Have students work with a partner to complete the sentences. Call on volunteers to read the completed sentences aloud.

3. Have the pairs read the sentences together.

Vocabulary Answers, p. 67
1. camp;
2. effect;
3. distance;
4. Suddenly;
5. hole;
6. amazing;
7. alive;
8. painful

 For additional practice with the vocabulary, have students visit *Q Online Practice*.

▶ *Listening and Speaking 1, page 68*

PREVIEW LISTENING 1 (5 minutes)

1. Direct students to look at the photo. Say: *This man's name is Joe Simpson. He's a mountain climber.* Ask if anyone has heard of him or has seen the film about him, *Touching the Void.*

2. Read the introduction and the answer choices aloud. Have students check their answer.

3. Tell students they should review their answer after the listening.

> **Preview Listening 1 Answer, p. 68**
> Checked: He fell and broke his leg but was able to return to camp.

Listening 1 Background Note

In 1988, Joe Simpson wrote a popular book about this experience called *Touching the Void.* It was made into a film of the same name in 2003. In the years since the accident, both Simpson and Yates have continued to climb and write about climbing.

LISTEN FOR MAIN IDEAS (5 minutes)

 CD1, Track 38

A (5 minutes)

1. Ask students to read the sentence parts.

2. Play the audio and have students complete the activity individually.

3. Elicit the answers from the class.

> **Listen for Main Ideas Answers, p. 68**
> **1.** d; **2.** f; **3.** g; **4.** a; **5.** e; **6.** b; **7.** c

B (5 minutes)

Have partners turn to page 201 and read the story together.

LISTEN FOR DETAILS (10 minutes)

 CD1, Track 39

1. Direct students to read the statements before they listen again.

2. As you play the audio, have students listen and mark the statements *T* or *F*.

3. Have students compare answers with a partner.

4. If necessary, replay the audio so that students can check their answers.

5. Go over the answers with the class. Elicit corrections for the false statements.

> **Listen for Details Answers, pp. 68–69**
> **1.** F; **2.** T; **3.** T; **4.** F; **5.** T; **6.** F; **7.** F; **8.** T

 For additional practice with listening comprehension, have students visit *Q Online Practice*.

▶ *Listening and Speaking 1, page 69*

WHAT DO YOU THINK? (10 minutes)

1. Ask students to read the questions and reflect on their answers.

2. Seat students in small groups and assign roles: a group leader to make sure everyone contributes, a note-taker to record the group's ideas, a reporter to share the group's ideas with the class, and a timekeeper to watch the clock.

3. Give students five minutes to discuss the questions. Call time if conversations are winding down. Allow them an extra minute or two if necessary.

4. Call on each group's reporter to share ideas with the class.

> **What Do You Think? Answers, p. 69**
> 1. Bad events: Joe fell and broke his leg; he fell over the side of the mountain; he had no food or water; Happy endings: Joe fell in a soft place; he survived the fall; he was near camp; Simon hadn't left yet.
> 2. Because he thought they would both die if he didn't. Possible opinions: It was the right choice because Joe survived in the end and there was no other way to deal with the situation; it was the wrong decision because he almost killed his friend.

Learning Outcome

Use the learning outcome to frame the purpose and relevance of Listening 1. Ask: *What did you learn that will help you have a group discussion about a bad situation with a happy ending.* (Students heard a story about someone who overcame a very bad situation.)

Listening Skill: Using information questions to understand a story

(5 minutes)

1. Direct students to read the information about asking questions.

2. Check comprehension by asking questions: *What questions should you ask yourself while you're listening to a story?*

A (5 minutes)
 CD1, Track 40

1. Play the audio and ask students to write answers to the questions.

2. Elicit the answers, focusing on correct understanding over correct grammar.

> **Activity A Answers, p. 69**
> 1. two British mountain climbers, Joe Simpson and Simon Yates;
> 2. They climbed a mountain. Joe broke his leg. Joe slipped and fell off the mountain. He fell into a deep hole but climbed out and survived.
> 3. 1985;
> 4. the Andes Mountains in Peru (Siula Grande)

▶ *Listening and Speaking 1, page 70*

B (5 minutes)
 CD1, Track 41

1. Direct students to look at the photo and predict what they think the news story will be about. Then play the audio and have them take notes in their notebooks. Remind them that notes are not written in complete sentences.

2. Have students ask and answer the questions with a partner. Go over the answers as a class.

> **Activity B Answers, p. 70**
> 1. a 65-year-old Australian woman, Mary Nelson;
> 2. She went outside to check on her horses. A kangaroo jumped on her. Her favorite horse rescued her.
> 3. yesterday afternoon at 3:00;
> 4. a farm outside Sydney, Australia

 For additional practice with using information questions to understand a story, have students visit *Q Online Practice*.

LISTENING 2: Make Your Own Happy Ending

VOCABULARY (10 minutes)

1. Direct students to read the sentences and definitions.

2. Ask them to write each bold word next to the correct definition. Remind them to look for context clues.

3. Elicit the answers and have students repeat the bold words.

> **Vocabulary Answers, pp. 70–71**
> **a.** attitude;   **b.** secret;   **c.** accident;
> **d.** appreciate;   **e.** expert;   **f.** completely;
> **g.** get hurt;   **h.** remember

 For additional practice with the vocabulary, have students visit *Q Online Practice*.

▶ *Listening and Speaking 1, page 71*

PREVIEW LISTENING 2 (5 minutes)

1. Read the introduction. Point out the title of the book and ask: *Would you want to read this book?*

2. Have students read the answer choices and check their answer. Tell them they should review their answer after the listening.

> **Preview Listening 2 Answer, p. 71**
> Checked: Appreciate the positive things in your life.

Listening 2 Background Note

Although people usually believe they will be happier if they have more money, a better job, or a nicer place to live, research has shown that once basic needs are met, a large part of a person's happiness is not related to material things. There are hundreds of books on the market that provide advice on how to increase happiness. Most of them emphasize the importance of optimism and personal relationships.

LISTEN FOR MAIN IDEAS (5 minutes)

🔊 CD1, Track 42

1. Direct students to read the statements. Tell them they will circle one main idea.

2. Play the audio and have students complete the activity individually.

3. Call on a volunteer for the answer.

> **Listen for Main Ideas Answer, p. 71**
> Main Idea: 2

Tip for Success (1 minute)

1. Read the tip aloud.

2. Elicit the kinds of information each *Wh-* question should guide them to listen for. (*When:* hours, dates, days; *Where:* places, locations; *Who:* people's names; *Why:* reason; *What:* events)

LISTEN FOR DETAILS (5 minutes)

🔊 CD1, Track 43

1. Direct students to read the questions and answer choices before they listen again.

2. As you play the audio, have students listen and circle their answer choices.

3. If necessary, replay the audio so that the students can check their answers. Then go over the answers with the class.

> **Listen for Details Answers, pp. 71–72**
> **1.** b; **2.** a; **3.** c; **4.** c

 For additional practice with listening comprehension, have students visit *Q Online Practice*.

► *Listening and Speaking 1, page 72*

WHAT DO YOU THINK?

A (10 minutes)

1. Ask students to read the questions and reflect on their answers.

2. Seat students in small groups and assign roles: a group leader to make sure everyone contributes, a note-taker to record the group's ideas, a reporter to share the group's ideas with the class, and a timekeeper to watch the clock.

3. Give students five minutes to discuss the questions. Call time if conversations are winding down. Allow them an extra minute or two if necessary.

4. Call on each group's reporter to share ideas with the class.

> **Activity A Answers, p. 72**
> Possible answers:
> **1.** Students may have a story about making a new friend, finding a job or academic opportunity, getting a financial benefit, or escaping a bad situation.
> **2.** family, friends, school, home, neighborhood

B (5 minutes)

1. Have students continue working in their small groups to discuss the questions in Activity B. Tell them to choose a new leader, note-taker, reporter, and timekeeper.

2. Call on the new reporter to share the group's answers to the questions.

> **Activity B Answers, p. 72**
> Possible answers:
> **1.** Students may tell about a good or bad experience they had that changed their attitude.
> **2.** Both of the stories were about accidents that people survived.

Learning Outcome

Use the learning outcome to frame the purpose and relevance of Listenings 1 and 2. Ask: *What did you learn from the story of the mountain climbers and the conversation with Ellen Sharpe that will help you have a group discussion about bad situations with happy endings?* (Students learned that a person's attitude can have a big effect on whether they are happy or not. Students can consider this idea while preparing for their group discussion.)

Vocabulary Skill: Using the dictionary
(5 minutes)

1. Direct students to read the information and the dictionary entry.

2. Check comprehension: *What are the related words for effective? Are they all the same part of speech? Do they all mean the same thing as effective?*

Skill Note

Point out to students that learning related words can help them expand their vocabulary and knowledge of how the words are used. When you introduce new vocabulary words, make a point of showing how any common related words are used.

21ST CENTURY SKILLS

Dictionary skills are vital both in the classroom and in future professional settings. A non-native speaker studying or working in an English environment will often need to rely on a dictionary, both for written and oral communication. Students who have learned how to take full advantage of their dictionary have a vital tool for learning independence. Help students achieve this independence by emphasizing the dictionary skills they learn throughout the course and how these can assist them both academically and professionally. Point out that sometimes they may not find the word they're looking for in the dictionary because it's in the entry of a related word. They need to think about whether the word is in a conjugated verb form, a negative form, or a plural form.

▶ *Listening and Speaking 1, page 73*

A (5 minutes)

1. Direct students to look over the chart. Point out that a gray cell means that there is no related word for that part of speech.

2. Have students work individually to complete the chart.

3. Go over the answers with the class. As you correct, provide sample sentences for some of the related words. *It was an* accidental *meeting. I accidentally* texted the wrong person.

Activity A Answers, p. 73
2. amazement, amaze, amazed, amazingly;
3. organize;
4. confusion, confuse;
5. decide, decisively;
6. accidental, accidentally;
7. happiness, happily;
8. pain; painfully;
9. sudden

B (10 minutes)

1. Have students read the sentences with a partner and circle the correct word.

2. Elicit the answers from the class. Ask partners to read the sentences together.

Activity B Answers, p. 73
1. happy;   2. amazingly;   3. sudden;
4. painful;   5. effective;   6. organize;
7. decision; 8. accidentally

MULTILEVEL OPTION

Group lower-level students and assist them with the task, explaining how to identify the correct word. For example: *This word describes the noun* person, *so we know it has to be an adjective.*

Group higher-level students and assign each group a set of related words from the chart. Ask them to write a sentence with each word. Elicit and correct their sentences, focusing on the use of the words rather than other grammatical issues.

 For additional practice with related words, have students visit *Q Online Practice*.

▶ *Listening and Speaking 1, page 74*

SPEAKING

Grammar: *because* and *so* (5 minutes)

1. Read the information about using *because* and *so*.

2. Check comprehension by asking questions: *Which word do we use to introduce a reason? Which do we use to introduce a result?* Point out that *because* and *so* begin a clause that includes a subject and a verb.

3. Make several statements and ask students to complete them with *because* or *so* clauses. *I was hungry _____. I was tired _____.*

Skill Note

So, like *and*, *but*, and *or*, is a coordinating conjunction. It combines two independent clauses, and the order of the clauses cannot be changed. *Because*, like *when*, *although*, and *if*, is a subordinating conjunction which makes the clause it is attached to a dependent clause. The order of the clauses can be switched, but if the dependent clause comes first, the sentence needs a comma: *Because I have great friends, I feel happy.*

A (5 minutes)

1. Direct students to work independently to match the two parts of each sentence.

2. Call on volunteers to read the completed sentences aloud.

   Activity A Answers, p. 74
   1. c; **2.** a; **3.** d; **4.** b; **5.** f; **6.** e

Critical Thinking Tip (1 minute)

1. Read the tip aloud.

2. Tell students that the ability to distinguish differences allows them to make more educated decisions.

Critical Q: Expansion Activity

Distinguishing Differences

Point out to students that they use this skill daily in their English class when they distinguish between similar vocabulary items and grammar structures.

Have them distinguish between *because* and *so* by using the words to describe different situations. Bring in magazine pictures of people in different situations and give each picture to a small group. Tell the group to write one sentence with *so* and one with *because*. For example, if the picture is of a man in a nice car: *He has a nice car because he's rich. He has a nice car, so he's going to take good care of it.* When the groups finish, have them exchange pictures and sentences and repeat the process. Tell the new group their sentences must be different from the previous group's. Pass the pictures a third time and then have the last group share the picture and all six sentences with the class.

B (5 minutes)

 CD1, Track 44

1. Direct students to read the conversations and complete them with *because* or *so.*

2. Have partners compare answers. Play the audio so students can check their answers.

3. Go over the answers as a class.

   Activity B Answers, pp. 74-75
   1. so, because; **2.** so, because; **3.** because, so

C (5 minutes)

1. Have students read the conversations with a partner.

2. Ask volunteers to read the conversations aloud.

   For additional practice with *because* and *so*, have students visit *Q Online Practice.*

▶ *Listening and Speaking 1, page 75*

Pronunciation: Syllables and syllable stress (5 minutes)

CD1, Tracks 45, 46

1. Read the information about syllables.

2. Play the examples on the audio. Then have the students say the words and clap out the syllables.

3. Have students identify the stressed syllable in *SE·cret, com·PLETE·ly,* and *ef·FEC·tive·ly.*

Skill Note

Correct syllable stress is vital for speaking clear, natural English. When you teach new vocabulary, ask students to identify the number of syllables and the stressed syllable. Keep an ear open for syllables that students are dropping or stressing incorrectly. To reinforce this skill, have students underline the stressed syllables of important words before they read sentences or conversations together.

Listening and Speaking 1, page 76

A (5 minutes)

CD1, Track 47

1. Have students listen, repeat each word, and write the number of syllables.

2. Elicit the answers from volunteers. Elicit the stressed syllable and have the class repeat each word.

> **Activity A Answers, p. 76**
> **1.** 2; **2.** 4; **3.** 2; **4.** 3; **5.** 1; **6.** 3; **7.** 3; **8.** 3

B (5 minutes)

CD1, Track 48

1. Have students listen and circle the stressed syllable in each word.

2. Have the class repeat each word.

3. Call on volunteers to pronounce the words for the class.

> **Activity B Answers, p. 76**
> These syllables should be circled:
> **1.** hos; **2.** plete; **3.** se; **4.** fec;
> **5.** sud; **6.** at; **7.** trol; **8.** hap

 For additional practice with syllables and syllable stress, have students visit *Q Online Practice*.

Speaking Skill: Responding in a conversation (5 minutes)

1. Read the introduction.

2. Check comprehension: *Why should you say uh-huh? What can you say to show interest? How do you respond to bad news? To good news?*

3. Say and have students repeat all of the expressions.

Listening and Speaking 1, page 77

A (5 minutes)

CD1, Track 49

1. Direct students to read the conversation before you play the audio.

2. Play the audio. Have students listen and complete the conversation with the correct expressions.

3. Elicit the answers and write them on the board.

> **Activity A Answers, p. 77**
> **1.** Uh-huh, I see; **2.** Really?; **3.** Oh, no! How awful!;
> **4.** Wow!; **5.** Mm hmm. I see.

B (5 minutes)

1. Have partners read the conversation together. Monitor and assist with pronunciation of the expressions.

2. Ask volunteers to read the conversation aloud.

Listening and Speaking 1, page 78

C (5 minutes)

1. Model the activity with a volunteer. Choose one of your more verbal students and have him/her answer question 1 while you respond with the expressions from the Speaking Skill box.

2. Pair students and have them ask and answer the questions.

Tip for Success (3 minutes)

1. Read the tip aloud.

2. Elicit ways to ask for repetition and refer students to p. 38 if they have forgotten. Make a statement, e.g., *I would like to visit _____,* and tell students to ask you follow-up questions.

 For additional practice with responding in a conversation, have students visit *Q Online Practice*.

Unit Assignment: Have a group discussion

Unit Question (5 minutes)

Refer students back to the ideas they discussed at the beginning of the unit about what makes a happy ending. Cue students if necessary by asking specific questions about the content of the unit: *What bad things happened to Joe Simpson and Ellen Sharpe? How did their stories have happy endings?*

Learning Outcome

1. Tie the Unit Assignment to the unit learning outcome. Say: *The outcome for this unit is to participate in a group discussion about bad situations with happy endings. This Unit Assignment is going to let you show your skill in using because and so, using correct syllable stress, and responding in a conversation.*

2. Explain that you are going to use a rubric similar to their Self-Assessment checklist on p. 80 to grade their Unit Assignment. You can also share a copy of the Unit Assignment Rubric (on p. 45 of this *Teacher's Handbook*) with the students.

Consider the Ideas (5 minutes)

🔊 CD1, Track 50

1. Direct students to read the chart before you play the audio.

2. Play the audio. Ask students to check the bad situations and happy endings for each person.

3. Go over the answers as a class.

> **Consider the Ideas Answers, p. 78**
> Checked:
> **1.** She missed an interview because she got hurt.
> **2.** She decided to become a nurse.
> **3.** He failed a math test.
> **4.** He got into a good university and found a job he likes.

▶ *Listening and Speaking 1, page 79*

Prepare and Speak

Gather Ideas

A (10 minutes)

1. Direct students to write about bad situations with happy endings in the chart. Emphasize that they should write notes, not complete sentences. Demonstrate on the board by writing a complete sentence: *I was stuck at the airport for 15 hours, and I met someone there who became a good friend.* Elicit how much of the sentence would be written in the chart (*stuck at airport 15 hrs; met good friend*).

2. While students are working, monitor and provide feedback on their charts.

Organize Ideas

B (5 minutes)

1. Have students choose one situation and write sentences about it.

2. Monitor and provide feedback on students' use of *so* and *because*.

Speak

C (10 minutes)

1. Read the directions. Group students and remind them that the purpose is to have a discussion, not to read their sentences. Have students review the Self-Assessment checklist on p. 80 before they begin.

2. Use the Unit Assignment Rubric on p. 45 of this *Teacher's Handbook* to score each student. If you have a small class, have the groups conduct their discussions while the rest of the class listens so that you can complete the evaluations.

3. Alternatively, have partners evaluate each other. Distribute the Unit Assignment Rubric before the discussion. Tell them in advance whom they will be evaluating so that they pay special attention to that person.

Alternative Unit Assignments

Assign or have students choose one of these assignments to do instead of, or in addition to, the Unit Assignment.

1. Choose a story you have read or a movie you have seen where a bad situation turned out well. Take notes to prepare, and then tell the story to a group.

2. Interview five classmates to find out what they do when they want to cheer themselves up. For example, do they call a friend? Listen to music? Go for a walk? Present your information in groups.

🌐⁺ For an additional unit assignment, have students visit *Q Online Practice*.

▶ *Listening and Speaking 1, page 80*

Check and Reflect

Check

A (5 minutes)

1. Direct students to read and complete the Self-Assessment checklist on page 80.

2. Ask for a show of hands for how many students gave all or mostly *yes* answers.

3. Congratulate them on their success. Discuss the steps they can take if an item on the checklist was difficult for them. For example, if they had trouble responding in the conversation, they should review the expressions on p. 76 and practice using them in their casual conversations.

Reflect

Q **B** (5 minutes)

1. Refer students to the learning outcome on p. 81. Tell them to talk with their partners about whether they achieved the learning outcome.

2. Elicit the answers to the Unit Question that students came up with at the beginning of the unit.

3. Encourage them to flip through the unit as they discuss the new things they learned and new answers they may have to the Unit Question.

▶ *Listening and Speaking 1, page 81*

Track Your Success (5 minutes)

1. Have students circle the words they have learned in this unit. Suggest that students go back through the unit to review any words they have forgotten.

2. Have students check the skills they have mastered. If students need more practice to feel confident about their proficiency in a skill, point out the page numbers and encourage them to review.

3. Read the learning outcome aloud. Ask students if they feel that they have met the outcome.

Unit Assignment Rubric

Student name: _____

Date: _____

Unit Assignment: *Have a group discussion.*

20 points = Discussion element was completely successful (at least 90% of the time).
15 points = Discussion element was mostly successful (at least 70% of the time).
10 points = Discussion element was partially successful (at least 50% of the time).
 0 points = Discussion element was not successful.

Have a Group Discussion	20 points	15 points	10 points	0 points
Student spoke easily (without long pauses or reading) about a bad situation with a happy ending and was easy to understand (spoke clearly and at a good speed).				
Student used *because* and *so* correctly.				
Student used vocabulary from the unit.				
Student responded in conversations appropriately.				
Student stressed syllables in words correctly.				

Total points: _____

Comments:

Unit QUESTION
What is the best kind of vacation?

Vacation Time

LISTENING • understanding numbers and dates
VOCABULARY • suffixes *–ful* and *–ing*
GRAMMAR • *be going to*
PRONUNCIATION • reduction of *be going to*
SPEAKING • introducing topics in a presentation

LEARNING OUTCOME

Give a presentation describing a tour to a popular travel destination.

▶ *Listening and Speaking 1, pages 82–83*
Preview the Unit

Learning Outcome

1. Ask for a volunteer to read the unit skills, then the unit learning outcome.

2. Explain: *This is what you are expected to be able to do by the unit's end. The learning outcome explains how you are going to be evaluated. With this outcome in mind, you should focus on learning these skills (Listening, Vocabulary, Grammar, Pronunciation, Speaking) that will support your goal of giving a presentation about a tour to a travel destination. This can also help you act as mentors in the classroom to help the other students meet this outcome.*

A (10 minutes)

1. To get students thinking about the topic, ask: *Where do people like to go on vacation?* Make a list of places on the board.

2. Put students in pairs or small groups to discuss the first two questions.

3. Call on volunteers to share their ideas with the class. Ask questions: *Did you go sightseeing on your last vacation? Or did you just relax?* Explain what you do when you go sightseeing.

4. Focus students' attention on the photo. Have a volunteer describe the photo to the class.

5. Read the third question aloud. Ask students to explain why they would or wouldn't enjoy the vacation in the photo.

Activity A Answers, p. 83
Possible answers:
1. I went to Mexico. I visited my aunt in Seoul.
2. Students may mention famous cities, landmarks, or types of places such as beaches or temples.
3. Students might say they would enjoy the vacation in the photo because they like nature or they like to exercise; they might not enjoy it because it's too much work, they don't like dealing with insects and weather, or they don't like to be away from people.

B (15 minutes)

1. Introduce the Unit Question, *What is the best kind of vacation?* Label four pieces of poster paper (*Relaxing, Tourism, Nature, Other*) and place them in the corners of the room.

2. Ask students to read and consider the Unit Question for a moment and then stand in the corner next to the poster that best represents their answer to the question.

3. Direct the groups in each corner to talk amongst themselves about why they chose the answer they did. Tell them to choose a secretary to record ideas on the poster paper.

4. Call on volunteers from each corner to share the ideas with the class. Discuss whether any of the kinds of vacations students like could fall under more than one category.

5. Leave the posters up for students to refer back to at the end of the unit.

Activity B Answers, p. 83
Possible answers: Lower-level students may answer with a short phrase: *Relaxing vacations, Tourism vacations.* Mid-level students can expand with a brief explanation of why they like a particular kind of vacation: *Relaxing vacations relieve stress. Tourism vacations are interesting.* Higher-level students can expand on their opinions: *On a tourism vacation, you learn something, and you can enjoy museums and historical sites. Nature vacations are beautiful, and they provide opportunities to exercise and see wildlife.*

The Q Classroom (5 minutes)
CD2, Track 2

1. Play The Q Classroom. Use the example from the audio to help students continue the conversation. Ask: *How did the students answer the question? Do you agree or disagree with their ideas? Why?*

2. Ask which corner they think the students on the audio would have stood in and why.

EXPANSION ACTIVITY: Dream Vacation (10 minutes)

1. Tell students to imagine their dream vacation. Write these questions on the board: *Where are you going? Who are you going with? How are you going to spend your days? How are you going to spend the evenings?* Ask them to think about but not write their answers.

2. Have the students stand and mingle, asking each other about their dream vacations using the questions on the board. Participate in the activity.

▶ *Listening and Speaking 1, page 84*

C (10 minutes)

1. Direct students to look at the signs. Elicit the location of the first group of signs (near water) and the meaning of several of the signs.

2. Have students work with a partner to write the location and meaning of the signs.

3. Elicit answers from volunteers.

Activity C Answers, p. 84
1. location: near water/a lake/an ocean/a river; no swimming, no littering, no fishing, no diving, no boating, no lifeguard;
2. location: park or recreational area; no camping, no pets, don't pick the flowers, no glass bottles, no fires, no off-road vehicles;
3. location: museum or historic site; no food, no smoking, no pictures, no cell phones, no umbrellas, no skating or rollerblading

D (10 minutes)

1. Have each pair from Activity C sit with another pair to discuss the questions.

2. Call on volunteers to share each group's ideas with the class. If any students drew an interesting sign in their group, ask them to share and explain the drawing.

Activity D Answers, p. 84
Possible answers:
1. for safety, to keep the areas clean;
2. Yes, because people need to know the rules; No, because some of the rules should be obvious.
3. Students may have seen unusual signs in their community or on the roadways.

LISTENING

▶ *Listening and Speaking 1, page 85*

LISTENING 1: Places in Danger

VOCABULARY (10 minutes)

1. Direct students to read the words and definitions in the box. Pronounce and have students repeat the words.

2. Have students work with a partner to complete the sentences. Call on volunteers to read the completed sentences aloud.

3. Have the pairs read the sentences together. Elicit any related words that students know, e.g., *danger, electricity, pollute, tourism.*

MULTILEVEL OPTION

Group lower-level students and assist them with the task. Provide alternate example sentences to help them understand the words. For example: *Where is our **local** library? We can't swim in that water because of the **pollution**. Don't **shake** your soda can! We get a lot of **tourists** in this city.*

Have higher-level students complete the activity individually and then compare answers with a partner. Tell the pairs to write an additional sentence for each word. Have volunteers write one of their sentences on the board. Correct the sentences with the whole class, focusing on the use of the words rather than other grammatical issues.

Vocabulary Answers, p. 85
1. local; **2.** shake; **3.** destroy; **4.** pollution;
5. tourists; **6.** dangerous **7.** insect; **8.** electric

 For additional practice with the vocabulary, have students visit *Q Online Practice*.

▶ *Listening and Speaking 1, page 86*
PREVIEW LISTENING 1 (5 minutes)

1. Direct students to look at the photos. Ask what they know about the three places. Ask which one they would like to go to.

2. Read the introduction. Elicit guesses for why the places are in danger and write their ideas on the board. Tell students to review their ideas after the listening.

Preview Listening 1 Answers, p. 86
1. pollution; **2.** non-native insects;
3. vehicles shaking the ground

Listening 1 Background Note

Indian authorities have been trying to protect the Taj Mahal from pollution for many years. In the most recent effort, a "mud pack" was applied to the building to remove impurities and restore its white surface. The treatment aroused some controversy, with some saying it was effective and others saying that it caused uneven coloring.

The Galapagos Islands are home to many unique plants and animals. One is the giant tortoise for which the islands were named. In addition to the dangerous insects brought by tourists, many species of non-native plants and animals (including goats, cats, and dogs) are destroying the habitats of the native populations.

The Great Pyramid of Giza was the tallest man-made structure in the world for over 3,800 years. For much of its long life, it was covered with white limestone blocks, but these were removed hundreds of years ago, leaving the pyramid vulnerable to weathering. The inside of the pyramid has also been damaged by heavy tourism, and now authorities allow no more than 300 visitors a day inside the pyramid.

LISTEN FOR MAIN IDEAS (5 minutes)

 CD2, Track 3

1. Direct students to read the items and the answer choices.

2. Play the audio and have students complete the activity individually.

3. Call on volunteers to read the completed statements aloud.

Listen for Main Ideas Answers, p. 86
1. c; **2.** a; **3.** b

▶ *Listening and Speaking 1, page 87*
LISTEN FOR DETAILS (5 minutes)

 CD2, Track 4

1. Direct students to read the sentences before they listen again.

2. As you play the audio, have students listen and circle the correct word to complete each sentence.

3. Have students compare answers with a partner.

4. Replay the audio so that the partners can check their answers.

5. Go over the answers with the class.

Listen for Details Answers, p. 87
1. wife; **2.** cars; **3.** animals;
4. insects; **5.** age; **6.** walk

 For additional practice with listening comprehension, have students visit *Q Online Practice*.

WHAT DO YOU THINK? (10 minutes)

1. Ask students to read the questions and reflect on their answers.

2. Seat students in small groups and assign roles: a group leader to make sure everyone contributes, a note-taker to record the group's ideas, a reporter to share the group's ideas with the class, and a timekeeper to watch the clock.

3. Give students five minutes to discuss the questions. Call time if conversations are winding down. Allow them an extra minute or two if necessary.

4. Call on each group's reporter to share ideas with the class.

> **MULTILEVEL OPTION**
>
> Assign groupwork tasks according to the level of your students. Have higher-level students be group leaders and recorders and have lower-level students serve as timekeepers.

What Do You Think? Answers, p. 87

Possible answers:

1. Yes, I was surprised because I'd never heard about the problems before; No, I wasn't surprised because tourists always cause damage.

2. Students may suggest limiting the number of tourists, closing sites for recreation, raising prices so fewer people go, or building fences around the pyramids and the Taj Mahal.

3. If students are unaware of tourism damage to the places in their countries, suggest that they research the topic on the Internet and report back to the class the next day.

Learning Outcome

Use the learning outcome to frame the purpose and relevance of Listening 1. Ask: *What did you learn from Listening 1 that will help you give a presentation about a tour to a popular travel destination?* (Students learned about some problems in popular travel destinations. They can take these into consideration when presenting their own travel destination.)

Listening Skill: Understanding numbers and dates (15 minutes)

CD2, Tracks 5, 6, 7

1. Direct students to read the information about stress patterns in numbers.

2. Play the audio of the pairs of numbers.

3. Check comprehension. Write numbers on the board as words: *fifteen, fifty, thirteen, thirty,* etc. Elicit and underline the stressed syllable.

4. Write numbers in two columns, column 1: *13, 14, 15,* etc. and column 2: *30, 40, 50,* etc. Pronounce a number and ask students to hold up one finger for column 1 and two for column 2. Then have them try it with a partner. Partner A says numbers at random and Partner B guesses the column.

5. Play the audio of the large numbers. Write similar numbers on the board: a. 450, b. 4,450, c. 40,500, d. 450,000, and e. 4,500,000. Say the numbers and have students identify them by letter. Then put up a new set of numbers and have them try it with a partner.

6. Play the audio of the dates. Call on students to say their birth year. If your students may be sensitive about revealing their ages, ask for the years of famous events, e.g., *What year were the Summer Olympics last held? What year is the next World Cup?*

▶ *Listening and Speaking 1, page 88*

A (10 minutes)

CD2, Track 8

1. Play the audio and direct students to listen and circle the numbers they hear.

2. Elicit the answers from the class and write them on the board. Then ask partners to read the paragraphs together.

Activity A Answers, p. 88
1. 1632; 20,000; 3,000,000; **2.** 19; 175,000;
3. 4,500; 137; 2,000,000

Tip for Success (1 minute)

1. Read the tip aloud.

2. Point out that listening to the news is an excellent way to practice because the information is likely to be familiar. If they already know about the news, they'll be able to pick out names, numbers, cognates, and familiar topics from the English newscast.

▶ *Listening and Speaking 1, page 89*

B (10 minutes)

CD2, Track 9

1. Have students look at the travel quiz. Elicit any information they know about the places pictured.

2. Direct students to complete the quiz with their best guesses. Play the audio and ask them to check their answers.

3. Have partners read the completed sentences.

Activity B Answers, p. 89
1. b; **2.** c; **3.** a; **4.** b; **5.** c; **6.** b; **7.** b; **8.** a

 For additional practice with listening for numbers and dates, have students visit *Q Online Practice*.

LISTENING 2: A Helpful Vacation
VOCABULARY (10 minutes)

1. Direct students to work with a partner to read the sentences and circle the definitions.

2. Go over the answers with the class. Elicit any context clues that helped define the words. For example, in number 2 *great pictures*, and in number 5 *pack my bags*.

> **Vocabulary Answers, p. 90**
> **1.** a;
> **2.** b;
> **3.** a;
> **4.** b;
> **5.** a;
> **6.** a;
> **7.** a;
> **8.** b

 For additional practice with the vocabulary, have students visit *Q Online Practice*.

PREVIEW LISTENING 2 (5 minutes)

1. Direct students' attention to the photos and ask what they see in each picture. Point out Peru on a map and elicit any information students know about it.

2. Read the introduction and have students check the activities they think they will hear.

3. Tell them they should review their answers after the listening.

> **Preview Listening 2 Answer, p. 91**
> Checked: 1, 2, 3

Listening 2 Background Note

Volunteer travel is a burgeoning field, and there are many organizations that coordinate this kind of travel to countries all over the world. Volunteer opportunities include working with children, the elderly, or women and doing environmental, agricultural, health care, or construction work. There are even some newlywed couples opting for a "volunteer honeymoon," spending their first vacation as a married couple helping others.

LISTEN FOR MAIN IDEAS (5 minutes)

 CD2, Track 10

1. Direct students to read the items.

2. Play the audio and have students complete the activity individually.

3. Elicit the answers from the class.

> **Listen for Main Idea Answers, p. 91**
> Checked: b, c, e, h, i

LISTEN FOR DETAILS (10 minutes)

 CD2, Track 11

1. Direct students to read the statements and answer choices before they listen again.

2. As you play the audio, have students listen and choose the correct answer.

3. Have students compare answers with a partner.

4. Go over the answers with the class.

5. Ask partners to read the completed statements.

> **Listen for Details Answers, p. 92**
> **1.** b;
> **2.** c;
> **3.** a;
> **4.** a;
> **5.** c;
> **6.** b

 For additional practice with listening comprehension, have students visit *Q Online Practice*.

WHAT DO YOU THINK?

A (10 minutes)

1. Ask students to read the questions and reflect on their answers.

2. Seat students in small groups and assign roles: a group leader to make sure everyone contributes, a note-taker to record the group's ideas, a reporter to share the group's ideas with the class, and a timekeeper to watch the clock.

3. Give students five minutes to discuss the questions. Call time if conversations are winding down. Allow them an extra minute or two if necessary.

4. Call on each group's reporter to share ideas with the class.

Activity A Answers, p. 92

Possible answers:

1. Students may say it sounds exciting because you travel to unusual places, learn about other cultures, and get to help others. They may say it's not exciting because it's work, and you may be exposed to poverty and other troubling situations.

2. Yes, because I want to help others; No, I prefer to relax on my vacations.

3. Teach children, help the elderly or women, assist doctors and nurses, plant trees, clean up polluted areas, build houses or schools. Students may also have particular skills they could use to help— engineering, health care, construction, etc.

▶ *Listening and Speaking 1, page 93*

B (5 minutes)

1. Have students continue working in their small groups to discuss the questions in Activity B and complete the chart.

2. Call on the reporter to share each group's answers. Create a class chart for question 1.

3. For question 2, if students don't know the answer, ask them to search online.

Activity B Answers, p. 93

Possible answers:

1. Good: you learn about other cultures, you gain a better understanding of the world; Bad: tourists can cause damage, they can carry harmful plants and animals.

2. Students may say that tourists can build houses, work in schools or hospitals, plant trees, or help clean up pollution.

Learning Outcome

Use the learning outcome to frame the purpose and relevance of Listenings 1 and 2. Ask: *What did you learn from Listenings 1 and 2 that will help you present a tour to a popular travel destination?* (Students learned that travelers can both harm places and help them. Students may want to take this into account when presenting their tour and destination.)

Vocabulary Skill: Suffixes *-ful* and *-ing* (5 minutes)

1. Read the information about suffixes.

2. Check comprehension: *What suffix can you use to change a noun into an adjective? a verb into an adjective?*

3. Point out that these suffixes can be used with many but not all verbs and nouns.

Skill Note

Additional *-ful* adjectives include: *powerful*, *truthful*, *harmful*, *tasteful*, *painful*, *helpful*, *thoughtful*, and *useful*. Some *-ing* adjectives that might be useful for the Unit Assignment include: *charming*, *comforting*, *entertaining*, *fascinating*, *inspiring*, *relaxing*, *surprising*, and *thrilling*.

A (5 minutes)

1. Direct students to complete the sentences with the adjective form of the verbs in parentheses.

2. Ask volunteers to read the completed sentences aloud.

Activity A Answers, pp. 93–94
1. amazing; **2.** peaceful; **3.** helpful;
4. charming; **5.** meaningful; **6.** rising;
7. interesting; **8.** careful

B (10 minutes)

Read the directions and have students work individually to write their sentences. If you have students who have never visited a tourist place, provide the option of writing about any place they have been to.

Activity B Answers, p. 94
Possible sentences: Paris is a wonderful city. The Grand Canyon is amazing. Tokyo is very exciting. The beaches in Thailand are beautiful.

MULTILEVEL OPTION

Pair lower-level students for Activity A and allow them to help each other. Put the pairs in groups for Activity B and assist the groups as necessary with writing sentences.

C (5 minutes)

1. Read the directions and elicit additional follow-up questions. *How was the weather? How long did you stay? What was your favorite thing about it?* You may want to refer students to the information about asking follow-up questions on p. 19.

2. After students have completed the activity, call on volunteers to share information they learned about their partners.

 For additional practice with suffixes *–ful* and *–ing*, have students visit *Q Online Practice.*

SPEAKING

Grammar: *Be going to* (10 minutes)

1. Read the introductory information and the first bullet point about affirmative statements.

2. Tell students what you're going to do tomorrow. Elicit statements from volunteers about what they are going to do tomorrow and tell other students to listen carefully.

3. Call on individuals to restate what their classmates are going to do. *Berto is going to play soccer. Kim is going to study for her test.*

4. Read the second and third bullet points about negative statements and contractions. Repeat the above procedure, this time asking students to say what they are not going to do. Elicit third person statements from other students: *Mee Soon isn't going to study tonight.*

5. Read the bullet points about question formation. Then call on volunteers to ask you *yes/no* questions about next weekend. After you've answered, call on other volunteers to ask you follow-up information questions with *be going to.*

Skill Note

Emphasize to students that *be going to* is the future form most commonly used to discuss plans. Some students have a tendency to overuse *will* for future because it's a simpler form. When you hear this, remind them to choose *be going to* for plans. Point out the use of *be going to* for future plans when it occurs in listening activities.

A (10 minutes)

1. Direct students to look at the photo. Ask: *Where is this?*

2. Ask students to work individually to complete the sentences with the correct form of *be going to.* Remind them to use contractions.

3. Put students in pairs to compare answers. Ask them to read the email aloud together.

Activity A Answers, p. 96

1. 'm going to join;   2. 're going to do;
3. 're going to take;   4. 's going to be;
5. 're going to spend;   6. is going to teach;
7. is going to stop;   8. 's going to be;
9. 'm going to write

B (5 minutes)

🔊 CD2, Track 12

1. Direct students to match the questions and answers. Play the audio and have them check their answers.

2. Call on pairs of students to read the questions and answers aloud.

Activity B Answers, pp. 96–97

1. e;   2. d;   3. a;   4. c;   5. b

C (5 minutes)

1. Direct students to work individually to write the questions.

2. Have students ask and answer the questions with a partner.

3. Call on volunteers to talk about their partners' answers: *Bing is going to visit her sister this weekend.*

Activity C Answers, p. 97

2. Are you going to study English this weekend?
3. What are you going to do during the next holiday?
4. Where are you going to travel next summer?

 For additional practice with *be going to*, have students visit *Q Online Practice.*

Pronunciation: Reduction of *be going to*
(5 minutes)

🔊 CD2, Track 13

1. Read the introduction and play the audio.

2. Have students repeat each sentence. Point out the note about *gonna* not being used in writing.

3. Check comprehension. Write several simple statements on the board. *I'm going to eat dinner at 7:00. She's going to call her mom tonight. They're going to wake up early.*

4. Call on students to read each sentence, using *gonna.*

A (10 minutes)

1. Direct students to write answers to the questions. Monitor and correct use of *be going to*.

2. Have students ask and answer the questions with a partner.

3. Monitor and provide feedback on the reduced pronunciation of *going to*. Listen for students making the common error of saying *gonna to*.

4. For more practice, have students go back to grammar activities B and C and say the sentences there, using *gonna*.

> **Activity A Answers, p. 98**
> Written answers should be complete sentences with *I'm going to*. Spoken questions/answers include *gonna*.

B (10 minutes)

1. Before students begin the activity, review the possibilities for volunteer tourism—the kinds of places they could visit and activities that volunteers could do.

2. Have students find a new partner (different from their partner for Activity A) and ask and answer the questions about their volunteer tour.

> **Activity B Answers, p. 98**
> Locations may include virtually any place in the world where people need help, including rural or inner-city areas of wealthy countries. Activities might include construction work, teaching, health care work, food delivery, or agricultural work.

 For additional practice with reduction of *be going to*, have students visit *Q Online Practice*.

Speaking Skill: Introducing topics in a presentation (5 minutes)

1. Read the information about introducing topics.

2. Have students repeat each phrase. Provide examples for each phrase: *Let's start with some background information. Now I'm going to explain the schedule*, etc.

3. Check comprehension: *How can we introduce the first topic? How can we change to a new topic?*

Critical Thinking Tip

1. Read the tip aloud.

2. Tell students that when they decide on something, they should think about the advantages or disadvantages of the choice they will make.

A (5 minutes)

Pair students and have them number the topics from 1 to 6.

> **Activity A Answers, p. 99**
> Presentation order will vary from student to student.

B (5 minutes)

1. Ask the partners from Activity A to take turns saying sentences using the expressions from the Speaking Skill box and the topics in Activity A.

2. Call on volunteers to say their sentences.

3. Point out that it's important to emphasize these transitions so that listeners don't miss them. Encourage students to emphasize *First, Now, Next, Finally*, and *To wrap up* with slow, clear pronunciation and a pause before and after.

> **Activity B Answers, p. 99**
> Any of the expressions from the Speaking Skill box can be combined with any of the topics in Activity A. Students should use the expressions in the correct order.

 For additional practice with introducing topics in a presentation, have students visit *Q Online Practice*.

21ST CENTURY SKILLS

Teaching students how to introduce topics helps them move beyond simple communication and into the realm of organizing their ideas. Whether they are speaking in a classroom or at a business meeting, the ability to organize and present their ideas coherently is essential. These small speech markers can help students develop organizational skills because using them forces students to ask themselves two important questions: 1) *What are the topics I want to talk about?* and 2) *In what order do I want to present them?*

Unit Assignment: Plan and present a travel tour

Unit Question (5 minutes)

Refer students back to the ideas they discussed at the beginning of the unit about what the best kind of vacation is. Have them look at the four posters they created at that time and ask if they have anything to add now. Cue students if necessary by asking specific questions about the content of the unit: *What did we learn about the effects of tourism? About volunteer travel?*

Learning Outcome

1. Tie the Unit Assignment to the unit learning outcome. Say: *The outcome for this unit is to give a presentation describing a tour to a popular travel destination. This Unit Assignment is going to let you show your skill in introducing topics and in using* be going to *and* gonna.

2. Explain that you are going to use a rubric similar to their Self-Assessment checklist on p. 100 to grade their Unit Assignment. You can also share a copy of the Unit Assignment Rubric (on p. 56 of this *Teacher's Handbook*) with the students.

Consider the Ideas (5 minutes)

◉)) CD2, Track 14

A (5 minutes)

1. Play the audio and ask students to number the topics.

   Activity A Answers, p. 99
   1, 3, 2, 5, 4

B (10 minutes)

◉)) CD2, Track 15

1. Replay the audio and ask students to take notes in their notebooks.

2. Have them compare notes with a partner.

3. Call on volunteers to share their notes with the class.

4. Elicit any transition phrases they heard. (*Let's start with; Now let's move on; Now Lisa is going to tell you; Next, I'm going to talk about; Now Doug is going to take over; To wrap up*)

Activity B Answers, p. 99
Schedule: 14 days, March 9-March 22; Lodging: hotel, camping; Activities: hiking, camping, learning about plants and animals, planting trees; Food: local dishes—meat or rice curry with vegetables; Cost: $2,700

▶ *Listening and Speaking 1 page 100*

Prepare and Speak

Gather Ideas

A (10–20 minutes)

1. Group students and have them choose a place that all or most of them are familiar with. Remind them that their notes should not be in complete sentences.

2. If students are going to do research, tell them to take notes on the information they get, but not to copy source material word for word.

3. If most of the class is going to be doing research, conduct a short lesson on plagiarism. Project or photocopy a short paragraph from an online travel guide and walk students through the process of noting down essential information and paraphrasing. Encourage students to put source materials away and write about what they remember—this will help them use their own words.

Organize Ideas

B (15–20 minutes)

1. Instruct the groups to plan what each person will talk about. Have them print out images from the Internet or bring photos from home as a visual aid.

2. Assign a time limit (10 minutes) for each group and appoint a timekeeper to help them stay on task.

Tip for Success (1 minute)

1. Ask students to read the tip aloud.

2. Point out that these phrases are for politely interrupting to add information or say something you forgot.

Speak

C (15–20 minutes)

1. Direct students to review the Self-Assessment checklist before giving their presentations. Then have groups practice their presentations. Monitor and provide feedback on the introduction of new topics.

2. Use the Unit Assignment Rubric on p. 56 of this *Teacher's Handbook* to score each student's part of the presentation.

3. Alternatively, have each group present to another group. Have listeners complete the Unit Assignment Rubric.

Critical Q: Expansion Activity

Deciding on a Sequence

Deciding on a sequence requires the skills of analysis and evaluation. Have students practice these skills by using the travel information presented by their classmates. Tell the class they have three months of vacation coming up and money to spend on three of the tours they heard about from their classmates.

Tell them to decide which three trips they will take and in what order. They should take into account preparation required, location, and activities involved.

Alternative Unit Assignments

Assign or have students choose one of these assignments to do instead of, or in addition to, the Unit Assignment.

1. Think about good places for tourists to visit in your country. Choose one place and make a poster about it. Where is the place? What activities can tourists do there? Present your poster in a small group.

2. Visit a travel agency or use the Internet to find out about different volunteer tours. Choose one you think is interesting and tell the class about it.

 For an additional unit assignment, have students visit *Q Online Practice*.

Check and Reflect

Check

A (5 minutes)

1. Direct students to read and complete the Self-Assessment checklist.

2. Ask for a show of hands for how many students gave all or mostly *yes* answers.

3. Congratulate them on their success. Discuss the sections of the unit they should refer to if an item on the checklist was difficult for them. For example, if they had trouble with *be going to*, they should refer to pages 95–96.

Reflect

B (5 minutes)

1. Refer students to the learning outcome on p. 101. Tell them to talk with their partners about whether they achieved the learning outcome.

2. Elicit the answers to the Unit Question that students came up with at the beginning of the unit.

3. Encourage them to flip through the unit as they discuss the new things they learned and new answers they may have to the Unit Question.

▶ *Listening and Speaking 1, page 101*

Track Your Success (5 minutes)

1. Have students circle the words they have learned in this unit. Suggest that they go back through the unit to review any words they have forgotten.

2. Have students check the skills they have mastered. If students need more practice to feel confident about their proficiency in a skill, point out the page numbers and encourage them to review.

3. Read the learning outcome aloud. Ask students if they feel that they have met the outcome.

Unit Assignment Rubric

Student name: _____

Date: _____

Unit Assignment: *Plan and present a travel tour.*

20 points = Presentation element was completely successful (at least 90% of the time).
15 points = Presentation element was mostly successful (at least 70% of the time).
10 points = Presentation element was partially successful (at least 50% of the time).
 0 points = Presentation element was not successful.

Plan and Present a Travel Tour	20 points	15 points	10 points	0 points
Student spoke easily (without long pauses or reading) about a travel destination and was easy to understand (spoke clearly and at a good speed).				
Student used *be going to* correctly.				
Student used vocabulary from the unit.				
Student clearly introduced new topics in the presentation.				
Student pronounced *be going to* correctly.				

Total points: _____

Comments:

LISTENING • listening for specific information
VOCABULARY • synonyms
GRAMMAR • simple present for informal narratives
PRONUNCIATION • simple present third-person *-s/-es*
SPEAKING • using eye contact, pause, and tone of voice

LEARNING OUTCOME

Use appropriate eye contact, tone of voice, and pauses to tell a funny story or a joke to your classmates.

▶ *Listening and Speaking 1, pages 102–103*
Preview the Unit

Learning Outcome

1. Ask for a volunteer to read the unit skills, then the unit learning outcome.

2. Explain: *This is what you are expected to be able to do by the unit's end. The learning outcome explains how you are going to be evaluated. With this outcome in mind, you should focus on learning these skills (Listening, Vocabulary, Grammar, Pronunciation, Speaking) that will support your goal of using appropriate eye contact, tone of voice, and pauses to tell a funny story or joke. This can also help you act as mentors in the classroom to help the other students meet this outcome.*

A (10 minutes)

1. To help students begin thinking about the topic, ask for a show of hands to see who likes to watch funny movies or comedies on TV. Ask how many read comic strips or have seen a comedian live.

2. Put students in pairs or small groups to discuss the first two questions.

3. Call on volunteers to share their ideas with the class. Ask questions: *Do you think American or British comedies are funny? Is it hard for you to tell jokes?*

4. Focus students' attention on the photo. Have a volunteer describe the photo to the class. Ask if they have seen it before or if they know where it's from. (It's Harold Lloyd in a scene from the 1923 silent comedy *Safety Last*. Although no longer

as popular as Charlie Chaplin or Buster Keaton, Lloyd was hugely popular in the 20s, and this scene is one of the most famous from silent comedy.)

5. Read the third question aloud and elicit students' responses.

Activity A Answers, p. 103
Possible answers:
1. Students' favorite comedies are likely to be from their own cultures. Encourage them to describe what the shows are about.
2. Yes, I make a lot of people laugh; No, I don't tell jokes, but I like jokes that other people tell.
3. The photo is funny because it's a crazy situation. It's not funny because it's too unreal (or because the man is in danger).

B (15 minutes)

1. Introduce the Unit Question, *Who makes you laugh?* Tell students to think about TV programs, movies, books, comics, newspapers, and friends and family. Say: *Let's start off our discussion by listing people that make us laugh.*

2. Seat students in small groups and direct them to pass around a piece of paper as quickly as they can, with each group member adding one item to the list. Tell them they have two minutes to make the lists, and they should add as many items as possible. They can write names of famous people, family members, or friends (*my uncle Cho, my friend Andre*), or descriptions (*the blonde woman on my favorite TV show*).

3. Call time and ask a reporter from each group to read the list aloud.

4. Use items from the list as a springboard for discussion. For example, *How do these people make you laugh? Do they tell jokes or do funny things? Do they make funny comments?*

Activity B Answers, p. 103
Possible answers: Lower-level students may provide names of professional comedians or people they know. Mid-level students may elaborate by explaining that they laugh because of embarrassing situations, physical comedy, witty dialog or comments, or because they can relate to the person/funny situation. Higher-level students may provide an anecdote of a situation when someone made them laugh.

The Q Classroom
CD2, Track 16

1. Play The Q Classroom. Use the example from the audio to help students continue the conversation.

2. Ask: *How did the students answer the question? Do you agree or disagree with their ideas? Why?*

▶ *Listening and Speaking 1, page 104*

C (10 minutes)

1. Direct students to look at the photo and read the directions.

2. Ask them to write their ideas on the lines. Tell them to write at least three ideas.

3. Read the example conversation. Then ask partners to discuss their ideas.

D (10 minutes)

1. Have students write their own answers in the chart.

2. Ask them to continue working with their partner from Activity C, taking turns asking for information and completing the chart. Students can use the sentence starter *Tell me the name of…*

MULTILEVEL OPTION

As partners complete the chart, have higher-level students give an explanation of why the person makes them laugh. *(He tells a lot of jokes. She always has funny stories.)*

EXPANSION ACTIVITY: Share Favorites (10 minutes)

1. Tell students they are going to describe a favorite comedy show, movie, or funny person to their classmates.

2. Write questions on the board and ask them to think about but not write the answers.

For a show or movie: *What's the name of the show/ movie? When is it on?* (or *When did you see it?*) *Who is in it? What's it about?*

For a person: *What's his/her name? How often do you see him/her? Why does he/she make you laugh?*

3. Give students time to think about their answers to the questions.

4. Have everyone stand, find a partner, and tell their partner about their show/person. After they have spoken to one partner, they should find a new partner and repeat the process. Continue until everyone has spoken to at least three partners.

LISTENING

▶ *Listening and Speaking 1, page 105*

LISTENING 1:
Jackie Chan—Action-Comedy Hero

VOCABULARY (15 minutes)

1. Direct students to read each sentence and write the bold word next to the correct definition.

2. Put students in pairs to compare answers. Elicit the answers from volunteers. Have students repeat the vocabulary words.

3. Ask questions to help students connect with the vocabulary: *Who is your favorite comedian? Is your car powerful? What is the last film you saw?*

MULTILEVEL OPTION

Group lower-level students and assist them with the task. Provide alternate example sentences to help them understand the words. For example, *A professional does work for money. I like to sing, but I'm not a professional. I just do it for fun. That song is a big hit. Everyone loves it.*

After higher-level students have completed the activity, tell the pairs to write a sentence for each word/expression. Have volunteers write one of their sentences on the board. Correct the sentences with the whole class, focusing on the use of the vocabulary rather than other grammatical issues.

Vocabulary Answers, p. 105

a. film; **b.** However; **c.** huge;

d. professional; **e.** comedians; **f.** powerful;

g. hit; **h.** sense of humor

 For additional practice with the vocabulary, have students visit *Q Online Practice.*

▶ *Listening and Speaking 1, page 106*

Tip for Success (1 minute)

1. Read the tip aloud.

2. Tell students that when they actively predict what they're going to hear, it increases their understanding.

PREVIEW LISTENING 1 (5 minutes)

1. Read the introduction. Direct students to look at the photos. Ask them to think about why people will say Jackie Chan is funny.

2. Elicit students' predictions and write several on the board. Tell them to look back at the predictions after they listen.

Preview Listening 1 Answers, p. 106
Possible answers: He makes funny faces. He says/does funny things.

Listening 1 Background Note

Some other interesting facts about Jackie Chan:

- In addition to his other talents, Chan has released a number of albums and has sung many of the theme songs for the films in which he has starred.

- Chan holds the Guinness World Record for "Most Stunts by a Living Actor." Because he does all of his own stunts, it's difficult for him to get insurance for his productions. Over the years, he has dislocated his pelvis and broken his fingers, toes, nose, both cheekbones, hips, sternum, neck, ankle, and ribs on numerous occasions.

- Chan is an active and generous philanthropist and has worked for conservation and disaster relief and against animal abuse. He has two foundations which help needy young people in Hong Kong and other parts of China.

LISTEN FOR MAIN IDEAS (5 minutes)

 CD2, Track 17

1. Have students look over the topics.

2. Play the audio and ask them to number the topics in order.

3. Go over the answers as a class.

Listen for Main Ideas Answers, p. 106
1. f; **2.** a; **3.** c; **4.** e

LISTEN FOR DETAILS (5 minutes)

CD2, Track 18

1. Direct students to read the statements before they listen again.

2. As you play the audio, have students listen and circle the correct information to complete the sentences.

3. Go over the answers with the class.

Listen for Details Answers, p. 106
1. April; **2.** Hong Kong; **3.** acting career;
4. Hong Kong; **5.** not popular; **6.** 1998

For additional practice with listening comprehension, have students visit *Q Online Practice.*

▶ *Listening and Speaking 1, page 107*

WHAT DO YOU THINK? (10 minutes)

1. Ask students to read the questions and reflect on their answers.

2. Seat students in small groups and assign roles: a group leader to make sure everyone contributes, a note-taker to record the group's ideas, a reporter to share the group's ideas with the class, and a timekeeper to watch the clock.

3. Give students five minutes to discuss the questions. Call time if conversations are winding down. Allow them an extra minute or two if necessary.

4. Call on each group's reporter to share ideas with the class.

What Do You Think? Answers, p. 107

Possible answers:

1. because he smiles and laughs so much, because he's so fast, because he tells funny stories, because he has a great sense of humor;
2. Students may like Kung Fu movies because they are exciting and funny or may dislike them because they are violent and focus more on the action rather than on story or character development.
3. Students may talk about famous movies stars, TV stars, or stand-up comedians. They may be popular because they say and do funny things or because their humor appeals to many people.

Learning Outcome

Use the learning outcome to frame the purpose and relevance of Listening 1. Ask: *What did you learn from Listening 1 that will help you to tell a joke or funny story?* (Students learned what makes Jackie Chan funny: he smiles and laughs a lot. They can use these techniques when telling their joke or funny story.)

Listening Skill: Listening for specific information (3 minutes)

1. Direct students to read the information about listening for important details.
2. Explain that focusing on specific information can help listeners understand and retain what they hear. Point out that this is expanding on the Listening Skill in Unit 5 (pages 87–88).

A (5 minutes)

 CD2, Track 19

1. Direct students to read the information before they listen.
2. Play the audio and ask students to write the missing information.
3. Elicit the answers from the class.

> **Activity A Answers, p. 107**
> 1. April 7, 1954;
> 2. 1980s;
> 3. They loved him.
> 4. **a.** laughs a lot; **b.** fast; **c.** his fight scenes

▶ *Listening and Speaking 1, page 108*

B (5 minutes)

 CD2, Track 20

1. Direct students to read the paragraph.
2. Play the audio and have students complete the paragraph.
3. Have students compare their answers with a partner. Elicit answers from volunteers. Then ask partners to read the paragraph aloud together.

> **Activity B Answers, p. 108**
> 1. 2001; 2. 2005; 3. third; 4. 2009;
> 5. Tokyo, Japan; 6. comedy

For additional practice with listening for specific information, have students visit *Q Online Practice*.

Tip for Success (1 minute)

1. Ask students to read the tip aloud.
2. Point out that some radio program websites, such as the National Public Radio website, have text summaries and images that will help students understand as they listen.
3. Ask students what other kinds of media they could try this with. (Many TV networks put shows online after they air. Students can also borrow audio books from the library.)

▶ *Listening and Speaking 1, page 109*

LISTENING 2: Can Anyone Be Funny?

VOCABULARY (10 minutes)

1. Direct students to work with a partner. Ask pairs to read the sentences and circle the best definition for each bold word.
2. Call on volunteers to read each sentence and the definition they chose. Have the class repeat the bold words.
3. Have the pairs read the sentences together.

> **Vocabulary Answers, p. 109**
> 1. a; 2. b; 3. a; 4. b; 5. a; 6. a; 7. a; 8. a

 For additional practice with the vocabulary, have students visit *Q Online Practice*.

PREVIEW LISTENING 2 (5 minutes)

1. Direct students' attention to the photo. Tell them that a comedian who tells jokes on stage is called a stand-up comedian. Ask if they enjoy stand-up comedy.

2. Read the introduction. Ask students to think about the question and check the box that best represents their opinion.

3. Tell them they should review their answer after the listening.

> **Preview Listening 2 Answer, p. 110**
> Students' opinions will vary.

Listening 2 Background Note

Some additional advice for telling a funny story:

1. Be confident. People will want to listen to you if you are confident.

2. Ask your audience if they want to hear a funny story. Knowing the story is going to be funny will put people in the right frame of mind.

3. Make sure you remember all of the important details. Pausing to remember details can ruin the story.

4. Don't include irrelevant details, and keep the story short. People don't usually want to listen to long monologues.

5. Save the funniest part (the "punch line") for the end—if it is a surprise, it will be funnier.

LISTEN FOR MAIN IDEAS (5 minutes)

◗) CD2, Track 21

1. Direct students to read the unfinished statements and answer choices.

2. Play the audio and have students complete the activity individually.

3. Call on volunteers for the answers.

> **Listen for Main Ideas Answers, p. 110**
> **1.** b; **2.** b; **3.** c; **4.** a

LISTEN FOR DETAILS (5 minutes)

◗) CD2, Track 22

1. Direct students to read the statements.

2. As you play the audio, have students listen and mark the sentences *T* or *F.*

3. Have students compare answers with a partner.

4. Replay the audio so that the partners can check their answers.

5. Go over the answers with the class. Elicit corrections for the false sentences.

> **Listen for Details Answers, pp. 110-111**
> **1.** F; **2.** F; **3.** T; **4.** T; **5.** F; **6.** F

 For additional practice with listening comprehension, have students visit *Q Online Practice.*

Q WHAT DO YOU THINK?

A (10 minutes)

1. Ask students to read the questions and reflect on their answers.

2. Seat students in small groups and assign roles: a group leader to make sure everyone contributes, a note-taker to record the group's ideas, a reporter to share the group's ideas with the class, and a timekeeper to watch the clock.

3. Give students five minutes to discuss the questions. Call time if conversations are winding down. Allow them an extra minute or two if necessary.

4. Call on each group's reporter to share ideas with the class.

> **Activity A Answers, p. 111**
> Possible answers:
> **1.** Anyone can be funny if they follow advice for being funny (e.g., the advice from the listening); Being funny is a natural talent that cannot be learned.
> **2.** learn jokes, pay attention to things so that you can tell stories about them, smile and be confident while telling stories, think about the humorous part of embarrassing situations, laugh at yourself;
> **3.** Students might mention common joke topics (e.g., light bulb jokes).

B (5 minutes)

1. Have students continue working in their small groups to discuss the questions in Activity B. Tell them to choose a new leader, note-taker, reporter, and timekeeper.

2. Call on the new reporter to share the group's answers to the questions.

Activity B Answers, p. 111
Possible answers:

1. In a film: special effects and stuntmen can be used; the characters can redo a scene many times to make sure that it's as funny as possible; In a live theater: performers only have one chance to make their jokes or actions funny; there is an audience so performers can react to the audience's responses; The same principles for what makes people laugh apply in both: the unexpected, satire, physical comedy, witty dialog.

2. Students may say *yes* because laughing at yourself helps you not take your problems so seriously, makes you more fun to be around, and makes others laugh; they may say *no* because laughing at yourself may be embarrassing.

Learning Outcome

Use the learning outcome to frame the purpose and relevance of Listenings 1 and 2. Ask: *What did you learn from Listenings 1 and 2 that will help you tell a funny story?* Remind students that they should begin thinking about a funny story or joke they would like to tell for their Unit Assignment. (Students learned different ways that people can be funny.)

Vocabulary Skill: Synonyms (5 minutes)

1. Direct students to read the information and the dictionary entries silently.

2. Check comprehension: *What is a synonym? What is a synonym for* funny?

Skill Note

Because many synonyms have different usages or collocations, it's a good idea to focus on this skill as a receptive (listening and reading) skill, i.e., don't encourage students to always look up synonyms to use in their writing.

When you teach new vocabulary, elicit any synonyms that students already know. Have them practice with a card-exchange game. On each card, write a word that students will know a synonym for. Then give a card to each student. Have them mingle, asking, *What's a synonym for* _____? When they find a partner who can answer their question, they should exchange cards and move on to a new partner.

▶ *Listening and Speaking 1, page 112*

A (5 minutes)

1. Direct students to complete the activity individually, using their dictionaries if necessary.

2. Go over the answers with the class.

> **Activity A Answers, p. 112**
> **1.** huge;   **2.** funny;   **3.** famous;
> **4.** feelings;   **5.** laugh;   **6.** funny

B (10 minutes)

1. Have students work individually to find synonyms and write their sentences.

2. Suggest that students look up the entry for the synonym to see a more precise definition and an example sentence before they write their own sentence.

3. Demonstrate the reason for this. For example, students may find *monstrous* as a synonym for *huge*, but if they look up *monstrous*, they'll see that the first definition is *grotesque*, so it may not be an appropriate synonym in every circumstance.

4. Monitor students' work. If everyone is choosing the same synonym, suggest that some students choose the second or third option in their dictionaries.

> **Activity B Answers, p. 112**
> Possible synonyms:
> **1.** big, vast, immense, large, giant, gigantic;
> **2.** chuckle, guffaw, cackle, crack up;
> **3.** amusing, humorous, witty, hysterical

C (5 minutes)

1. Have students read their synonyms and sentences to a partner.

2. Call on volunteers to read their sentences aloud. Elicit any additional synonyms and sentences. For each word.

3. Explain any differences among the synonyms that might be important for understanding. For example, *vast* means *huge*, but it is usually used to describe a space or with words like *quantity* and *amount*.

 For additional practice with synonyms, have students visit *Q Online Practice.*

SPEAKING

Grammar: Simple present for informal narratives (5 minutes)

1. Read the information about using the simple present for informal narratives.

2. Explain that the simple present makes the story sound more immediate.

3. Have students repeat the simple present verbs in the story. Elicit the reason for the -*s* ending (third person singular).

Skill Note

It's important that students use the narrative simple present consistently because they will lose the desired effect if they keep switching from present to past. The main difficulty students will have with the narrative present is remembering to pronounce the third-person *s*, so monitor and provide feedback on pronunciation. Tell students to listen for the narrative present when they hear people telling stories.

A (10 minutes)

CD2, Track 23

1. Direct students to work individually to complete the jokes with the present tense verbs.

2. Play the audio so students can check their answers. Ask volunteers to read the jokes aloud.

3. Provide feedback on pronunciation. Elicit choral repetition of any difficult words.

> **Activity A Answers, pp. 113–114**
> **1: 1.** go; **2.** orders; **3.** brings; **4.** says;
> **5.** replies
> **2: 1.** is; **2.** asks; **3.** answers; **4.** thinks;
> **5.** says
> **3: 1.** stops; **2.** sees; **3.** tells; **4.** says;
> **5.** asks; **6.** looks

Critical Thinking Tip (2 minutes)

1. Read the tip aloud

2. Discuss things that people restate to others: jokes, stories, events, etc. Before students restate something, encourage them to think about the information they want to share and how they want to share it.

B (15 minutes)

1. Group students and tell them to divide the jokes so that each one will be told by at least one person. Give them time to study and remember the jokes.

2. Have them make notes on the lines and remind them not to write the whole joke.

3. Tell them to make a special note of the verbs so that they'll remember to pronounce the third-person -*s*.

4. Have students close their books and take turns telling their jokes, using simple present.

5. Monitor and make a note of which students need help with pronunciation.

 For additional practice with simple present for informal narratives, have students visit *Q Online Practice.*

Pronunciation: Simple present third person -*s*/-*es* (5 minutes)

CD2, Track 24

1. Read the information about third person -*s* and -*es*.

2. Provide additional examples, e.g., /z/: loves, knows; /s/: speaks, gets; /-es/ pushes, matches.

3. Play the audio and have students repeat.

Skill Note

Dropping the third person -*s* is a common pronunciation error. Students may not yet be at an appropriate stage to master this grammar. Continue to provide consistent modeling and correction for this error. Because it doesn't interfere with comprehension, students probably won't get feedback about it outside of class.

A (10 minutes)

1. Direct students to work individually to complete the task.

2. Have partners compare answers. Elicit answers from volunteers and write them on the board. Pronounce and have students repeat each verb.

Activity A Answers, p. 116

1. /s/ above –s: walks, asks, pets, bites;
/z/ above –s: sees, says, replies;

2. /s/ above –s: asks, starts, gets, takes;
/z/ above –s: says, pulls, replies, answers;
/əz/ above –es: pushes

B (10 minutes)

1. Pair students and have them read the jokes aloud.

2. Monitor and provide feedback on pronunciation.

 For additional practice with pronouncing third person -s/-es, have students visit *Q Online Practice*.

Tip for Success

1. Read the tip aloud

2. Elicit additional plural nouns that have final /s/, /z/, and /əz/ sounds.

▶ *Listening and Speaking 1, page 117*

Speaking Skill: Using eye contact, pause, and tone of voice (5 minutes)

 CD2, Track 25

1. Direct students to read the information about using eye contact, pauses, and tone of voice. Play the audio of the example.

2. Read the sample from the audio in a flat voice with no pauses while looking at the ground to demonstrate the importance of eye contact, pauses, and tone of voice.

3. Play the audio again and have students repeat the selection expressively.

21ST CENTURY SKILLS

The use of eye contact, pauses, and tone of voice is necessary not just for telling jokes, but for all dynamic speaking, both socially and professionally. Whether students are speaking in a job interview, giving a presentation, talking in a meeting, interacting with customers, or chatting with native English speakers, mastery of these skills will help them come across as confident and competent speakers.

In some cultures, lowering the eyes when speaking to an authority figure is considered a sign of respect. It's important that students understand that in many other countries, the opposite is true. Unwillingness to look someone in the eye may be interpreted as restlessness, dislike, or dishonesty.

A (10 minutes)

 CD2, Track 26

1. Direct students to read the excerpts before they listen.

2. Play the audio and have students mark the text.

3. Go over the answers with the class. You may want to project the page or make a transparency of it for ease of correction.

Activity A Answers, p. 117

1. Underline: *What are you doing; Nothing; You did that yesterday;* and *Yeah, I know. I wasn't finished.*
Pause arrow after *answer.*

2. Underline: *I hurt everywhere. It hurts when I touch my head. It hurts when I touch my leg, and it hurts when I touch my arm; I know what's wrong…Your finger is broken!* Pause arrow after *says.*

B (5 minutes)

1. Have partners take turns reading the excerpts.

2. Monitor their use of eye contact, tone of voice, and pauses.

▶ *Listening and Speaking 1, page 118*

C (10 minutes)

1. Have partners work together to mark the excerpts.

2. Monitor and provide feedback.

Activity C Answers, p. 118

1. Underline: *Excuse me. Your finger is in my soup;* and *Oh, that's OK. It isn't too hot.* Pause arrow after *replies.*

2. Underline: *Why do you have that penguin?; I told you to take it to the zoo;* and *Yes, thank you. I did that, and we had a great time! Today we're going to the movies!* Pause arrow after *says.*

D (10 minutes)

1. Have students take turns reading the excerpts.

2. Ask volunteers to read the excerpts for the class.

3. Provide feedback on use of eye contact, pauses, and tone of voice.

 For additional practice with using eye contact, pause, and tone of voice, have students visit *Q Online Practice*.

Q Unit Assignment: Tell a joke or a funny story

Unit Question (5 minutes)

Refer students back to the ideas they discussed at the beginning of the unit about who makes them laugh. Cue students if necessary by asking specific questions about the content of the unit: *Why did people think Jackie Chan was funny? What advice did we hear about how to be funny? What skills can you use to make your jokes and stories more entertaining?*

Learning Outcome

1. Tie the Unit Assignment to the unit learning outcome. Say: *The outcome for this unit is to use appropriate eye contact, tone of voice, and pauses to tell a funny story or a joke to your classmates. This Unit Assignment is going to let you show that you can do that as well as correctly use and pronounce the simple present.*

2. Explain that you are going to use a rubric similar to their Self-Assessment checklist on p. 120 to grade their Unit Assignment.

Critical Q: Expansion Activity

Synthesizing Information

Every Unit Assignment requires students to synthesize the information and skills they have learned throughout the unit. Help make this process more transparent to students by having them create a unit chart. List the elements of the unit at the top of the chart: Listening 1, Listening 2, Vocabulary, Grammar, Speaking Skill, Pronunciation. Have students copy the chart into their notebooks. As they prepare for their Unit Assignment, ask them to make a note in the chart of the different ideas/skills they are using from each section of the unit. Ask them to think about how they are using these skills for their Unit Assignment.

Consider the Ideas (10 minutes)

》 CD2, Tracks 27, 28

1. Direct students to work with a partner to read the joke and try to come up with a punch line.

2. Call on volunteers to share their ideas. Play the audio and ask students to write the punch line.

3. Play the audio again. Have partners discuss the questions and complete the task.

4. Call on volunteers to share if they understood the joke and why they thought the comedian was or wasn't good.

Consider the Ideas Answers, p. 119
1. Answers will vary;
2. "Well, that's the fastest way."
3. **a** & **b:** Students may or may not have understood the joke; this will likely affect their opinion about the comedian. **c:** The comedian changes his tone of voice whenever he says a line of dialog. The pause comes right before the punch line.

▶ *Listening and Speaking 1, page 119*

Prepare and Speak

Gather Ideas

A (10 minutes)

1. Tell students that it's time to tell the joke or funny story they have been thinking about during the unit.

2. If some students are stuck for ideas, ask other students to share their ideas to help inspire their classmates.

3. Remind students that their story can be an amusing anecdote about something one of their friends or family members did. It doesn't have to be a joke with a punch line.

Organize Ideas

B (15 minutes)

1. Have students work individually to make notes about their jokes or stories and to mark the places where they can pause or use tone of voice.

2. Monitor and provide feedback about the use of the present tense.

3. Remind students that practice is an important part of preparation. Have them practice their jokes/stories with a partner and give each other feedback on eye contact, tone of voice, and pauses.

MULTILEVEL OPTION

Group lower-level students and assist this group by providing feedback on their note-taking and practice. While you are working with the lower-level group, ask the higher-level students to practice their jokes or stories with several different partners.

C (10–15 minutes)

1. Direct students to look over the Self-Assessment checklist on p. 120. Remind students about making eye contact, pausing, using tone of voice, and using the simple present.

2. Call on students to tell their jokes or stories to the class.

3. Use the Unit Assignment Rubric on p. 67 of this *Teacher's Handbook* to score each student.

4. Alternatively, divide the class into large groups and have students tell their jokes/stories to their group. Have listeners complete the Unit Assignment Rubric.

Alternative Unit Assignments

Assign or have students choose one of these assignments to do instead of, or in addition to, the Unit Assignment.

1. Watch a comedy TV show in English. You can watch it on TV, DVD, or the Internet. Then tell the class about it. Was it funny? Why or why not?

2. What kinds of jokes are popular in your country? Tell the class some jokes from your culture. Are the jokes funny in English, too?

 For an additional unit assignment, have students visit *Q Online Practice*.

▶ *Listening and Speaking 1, page 120*

Check and Reflect

Check

A (5 minutes)

1. Direct students to read and complete the Self-Assessment checklist.

2. Ask for a show of hands for how many students gave all or mostly *yes* answers.

3. Congratulate them on their success. Discuss the steps they can take if an item on the checklist was difficult for them. For example, if they had trouble staying in the present tense, tell them to practice by recording themselves saying present-tense narratives and then listening to make sure they aren't dropping the -*s* or switching tenses.

Reflect

B (5 minutes)

1. Refer students to the learning outcome on p. 121. Tell them to talk with their partners about whether they achieved the learning outcome.

2 Elicit the answers to the Unit Question that students came up with at the beginning of the unit.

3. Encourage them to flip through the unit as they discuss the new things they learned and new answers they may have to the Unit Question.

▶ *Listening and Speaking 1, page 121*

Track Your Success (5 minutes)

1. Have students circle the words they have learned in this unit. Suggest that students go back through the unit to review any words they have forgotten.

2. Have students check the skills they have mastered. If students need more practice to feel confident about their proficiency in a skill, point out the page numbers and encourage them to review.

3. Read the learning outcome aloud. Ask students if they feel that they have met the outcome.

Unit 6 Laughter

Unit Assignment Rubric

Student name: _____

Date: _____

Unit Assignment: *Tell a joke or a funny story.*

20 points = Story or joke element was completely successful (at least 90% of the time).
15 points = Story or joke element was mostly successful (at least 70% of the time).
10 points = Story or joke element was partially successful (at least 50% of the time).
 0 points = Story or joke element was not successful.

Tell a Story or Joke	20 points	15 points	10 points	0 points
Student told the joke or funny story easily (without long pauses or reading) and was easy to understand (spoke clearly and at a good speed).				
Student used the simple present tense correctly.				
Student used vocabulary from the unit.				
Student used eye contact, pauses, and tone of voice to effectively tell the joke or funny story.				
Student correctly pronounced third person -s/-es.				

Total points: _____

Comments:

Unit QUESTION
Why is music important to you?

Music

LISTENING • listening for signal words
VOCABULARY • using the dictionary
GRAMMAR • gerunds as subjects or objects
PRONUNCIATION • questions of choice
SPEAKING • asking for and giving opinions

LEARNING OUTCOME

Participate in a group interview about how important music is in your lives.

▶ *Listening and Speaking 1, pages 122–123*
Preview the Unit

Learning Outcome

1. Ask for a volunteer to read the unit skills, then the unit learning outcome.

2. Explain: *This is what you are expected to be able to do by the unit's end. The learning outcome explains how you are going to be evaluated. With this outcome in mind, you should focus on learning these skills (Listening, Vocabulary, Grammar, Pronunciation, Speaking) that will support your goal of participating in a group interview about the importance of music. This can also help you act as mentors in the classroom to help the other students meet this outcome.*

A (10 minutes)

1. To help students begin thinking about the topic, elicit different kinds of music from the class (classical, folk, etc.). Write the kinds of music on the board.

2. Put students in pairs or small groups to discuss the first two questions.

3. Call on volunteers to share their ideas with the class. Ask questions: *When do you listen to music? Do you usually listen with an mp3 player, computer, or radio?*

4. Focus students' attention on the photo. Have a volunteer describe the photo to the class. Ask: *How old are the women? Where are they? Why do you think they are smiling?* Read the third question aloud and elicit students' answers.

Activity A Answers, p. 123
Possible answers:
1. all the time because I have an mp3 player and take it with me everywhere; when I study; at concerts;
2. classical, folk, or other genres particular to the students' countries;
3. listening to their favorite song; listening to a recording

B (15 minutes)

1. Introduce the Unit Question, *Why is music important to you?* Ask related information questions or questions about personal experience to help students prepare for answering the more abstract Unit Question. *How do you feel when you listen to music? Who do you listen to music with? Do you play an instrument?*

2. Put students in small groups and give each group a piece of poster paper and a marker.

3. Read the Unit Question aloud. Give students a minute to silently consider their answers to the question. Tell students to pass the paper and the marker around the group. Direct each group member to write a different answer to the question. Encourage them to help one another.

4. Ask each group to choose a reporter to read the answers to the class. Point out similarities and differences among the answers. If answers from different groups are similar, make a group list that incorporates all of the answers. Post the list to refer to later in the unit.

Activity B Answers, p. 123

Possible answers: Lower-level students may provide short answers: *It's relaxing; it makes me happy.* Mid-level students may use more detail: *Music helps me express myself; it's a connection to my family, friends, or culture; it's comforting; it helps me concentrate;* Higher-level students may be able to describe in more detail the role music has in their lives: *My family has always sung certain songs together on special occasions, and those songs are very meaningful to me.*

The Q Classroom

🔊 CD2, Track 29

1. Play The Q Classroom. Use the example from the audio to help students continue the conversation.

2. Ask: *How did the students answer the question? Do you agree or disagree with their ideas? Why?*

▶ *Listening and Speaking 1, page 124*

C (10 minutes)

🔊 CD2, Track 30

1. Direct students to look at the types of music.

2. Play the audio and have them number the types in the order they hear them.

3. Conduct a silent check for the answers. Call out the type of music and ask students to raise the number of fingers to represent the number they wrote next to each type.

4. If students misidentified any of the music types, replay the selections and discuss each one.

> **Activity C Answers, p. 124**
> **1.** Classical; **2.** Rock; **3.** Jazz; **4.** Pop

D (10 minutes)

1. Model the activity by reading the sample conversation with a volunteer. Help students form questions from the chart.

2. Direct students to stand up and find a different classmate to answer each question.

3. Participate in the activity and provide feedback.

MULTILEVEL OPTION

Allow lower-level students to ask just the *yes/no* questions.

Ask higher-level students to ask an additional follow-up question, e.g., *When did you start playing?* or *How often do you play?*

EXPANSION ACTIVITY:
Share Information (10 minutes)

1. After students have finished activity D, seat them in groups and have them share information about their classmates. For example, *Koji plays the guitar.*

2. Give each group a sheet of poster paper and direct them to write five sentences about classmates who are not in the group, e.g., *Koji, Maria, Tasha, and Kyunghee play musical instruments.*

3. Correct the sentences together.

E (5 minutes)

Call on individuals to share information they learned about their classmates.

LISTENING

▶ *Listening and Speaking 1, page 125*

LISTENING 1: Mind, Body, and Music

Tip for Success (1 minute)

1. Read the tip aloud.

2. Help students identify context clues in the first three sentences (*information, feelings; musician; make you feel happy and calm*).

VOCABULARY (15 minutes)

1. Direct students to read the sentences and write the bold words next to the correct definitions.

2. Put students in pairs to compare answers. Elicit answers from volunteers. Help students identify the context clues in each sentence.

3. Have students repeat the bold vocabulary words.

4. Ask partners to read the sentences together.

> **Vocabulary Answers, p. 125**
> **a.** lowers stress; **b.** concentrate; **c.** benefit;
> **d.** brain; **e.** instruments; **f.** active;
> **g.** improve; **h.** humans

 For additional practice with the vocabulary, have students visit *Q Online Practice*.

PREVIEW LISTENING 1 (5 minutes)

1. Direct students to look at the illustration. Ask: *What is the connection between music and our mind?*

2. Read the introduction and the answer choices aloud. Have students check their answers.

3. Tell students they should review their answers after the listening.

> **Preview Listening 1 Answers, p. 126**
> Checked: learning; memory; stress; physical problems

Listening 1 Background Note

In addition to the benefits mentioned in the audio, listening to music has been associated with improved motor skills, pain relief, and lowered blood pressure. Music education has also been associated with improved test scores, spatial relations, and hand-eye coordination.

LISTEN FOR MAIN IDEAS (5 minutes)

CD2, Track 31

1. Ask students to read the statements. Have them predict which ideas they will hear.

2. Play the audio and have students complete the activity individually.

3. Elicit the answers from the class.

> **Listen for Main Ideas Answers, p. 126**
> Checked: b, c, e, f

LISTEN FOR DETAILS (10 minutes)

CD2, Track 32

1. Direct students to read the questions and the answer choices before they listen again.

2. As you play the audio, have students listen and circle the correct answers.

3. Have students compare answers with a partner.

4. Replay the audio so that the partners can check their answers.

5. Have volunteers read the questions and answers for the class.

> **Listen for Details Answers, pp. 126-127**
> **1.** b; **2.** c; **3.** a; **4.** a; **5.** c

 For additional practice with listening comprehension, have students visit *Q Online Practice.*

Q WHAT DO YOU THINK? (10 minutes)

1. Ask students to read the questions and reflect on their answers.

2. Seat students in small groups and assign roles: a group leader to make sure everyone contributes, a note-taker to record the group's ideas, a reporter to share the group's ideas with the class, and a timekeeper to watch the clock.

3. Give students five minutes to discuss the questions. Call time if conversations are winding down. Allow them an extra minute or two if necessary.

4. Call on each group's reporter to share ideas with the class.

> **What Do You Think? Answers, p. 127**
> **1.** Yes, music helps me concentrate when I study; No, I prefer silence; I think classical music is best because it is relaxing.
> **2.** Yes, I listen to music after a long day at work/school because it helps me relax. I listen to music from my country when I am feeling homesick.
> **3.** Music has always been a part of people's lives; music can help with learning, concentration, and school performance; it helps with memory, physical problems, and stress; classical music activates the left and right side of the brain.

Learning Outcome

Use the learning outcome to frame the purpose and relevance of Listening 1. Ask: *What did you learn from Listening 1 that prepares you to interview a group about music?* (Students learned about some of the ways that music may be good for people. They can interview their group about some of these ideas.)

Listening Skill: Signal words and phrases (5 minutes)

1. Direct students to read the information about signal words and phrases.

2. Check comprehension by asking questions: *When do speakers use signal words? What signal words do they use at the beginning? In the middle? At the end?*

▶ *Listening and Speaking 1, page 128*

A (5 minutes)

 CD2, Track 33

1. Give students a minute to look over the sentences.

2. Play the audio and ask students to write the missing words.

3. Call on volunteers for the answers.

> **Activity A Answers, p. 128**
> **1.** The first important benefit;
> **2.** In addition;
> **3.** Another point is that;
> **4.** Finally

Tip for Success (1 minute)

1. Read the tip aloud.

2. Point out that these words signal points when students might want to start a new section in their notes, either by skipping a line or by numbering.

B (5 minutes)

1. Pair students to read the sentences from Activity A together.

2. Elicit any other signal words from page 127 that could fit in the sentences.

 For additional practice with signal words and phrases, have students visit *Q Online Practice*.

LISTENING 2: Music in Our Lives

VOCABULARY (10 minutes)

1. Direct students to read the words and definitions in the box. Pronounce and have students repeat the words.

2. Have students work with a partner to complete the sentences.

3. Call on volunteers to read the completed sentences aloud. Discuss the context clues in each sentence.

4. Have the pairs read the sentences together.

> **Vocabulary Answers, pp. 128-129**
> **1.** escape; **2.** rhythm; **3.** private; **4.** forget;
> **5.** team; **6.** tune; **7.** traditional; **8.** express

 For additional practice with the vocabulary, have students visit *Q Online Practice*.

▶ *Listening and Speaking 1, page 129*

PREVIEW LISTENING 2 (5 minutes)

1. Direct students' attention to the photos and ask: *How old are these people? Where do you think they are from?*

2. Have students read the introduction and match the statements to the photos.

3. Tell students they should review their answers after the listening.

> **Preview Listening 2 Answers, p. 129**
> **1.** b; **2.** d; **3.** c; **4.** a

Listening and Speaking 1, page 130

LISTEN FOR MAIN IDEAS (5 minutes)

 CD2, Track 34

1. Direct students to read the statements. Tell them they will check two statements for each person.

2. Play the audio and have students complete the activity individually.

3. Call on volunteers for the answers.

> **Listen for Main Ideas Answers, p. 129**
> **1.** a, c; **2.** b, c; **3.** a, c; **4.** a, b

LISTEN FOR DETAILS (10 minutes)

 CD2, Track 35

1. Direct students to read the questions before they listen again.

2. As you play the audio, have students listen and write answers.

3. Have students compare answers with a partner.

4. Replay the audio so that the partners can check their answers.

5. Go over the answers with the class.

> **Listen for Details Answers, pp. 130–131**
> Wording may vary.
> **1.** Maria listens to pop music.
> **2.** She practices dancing in the park with her friends.
> **3.** He likes to play and write rock and pop.
> **4.** Sometimes his guitar is his best friend.
> **5.** She prefers Japanese pop songs.
> **6.** Her parents listen to traditional Japanese music.
> **7.** Alex's favorite singer is from Brazil.
> **8.** He feels excited and ready to win.

 For additional practice with listening comprehension, have students visit *Q Online Practice*.

WHAT DO YOU THINK?

A (10 minutes)

1. Ask students to read the questions and reflect on their answers.

2. Seat students in small groups and assign roles: a group leader to make sure everyone contributes, a note-taker to record the group's ideas, a reporter to share the group's ideas with the class, and a timekeeper to watch the clock.

3. Give students five minutes to discuss the questions. Call time if conversations are winding down. Allow them an extra minute or two if necessary.

4. Call on each group's reporter to share ideas with the class.

> **Activity A Answers, p. 131**
> Possible answers:
> **1.** Yes, music energizes me too; I listen to it when I exercise.
> **2.** I am most similar to Jamal because I play the guitar, too.
> **3.** Music reminds me of happy times.

B (5 minutes)

1. Have students continue working in their small groups to discuss the questions in Activity B. Tell them to choose a new leader, note-taker, reporter, and timekeeper.

2. Call on the new reporter to share the group's answers to the questions.

> **Activity B Answers, p. 131**
> Possible answers:
> **1.** I think jazz is best for lowering stress because it's relaxing. I think classical is best for studying because it helps me concentrate. I think pop is best for exercising because it makes me want to dance.
> **2.** Students may mention traditional songs from their country, songs from their school days, or songs that remind them of friends or family.

Learning Outcome

Use the learning outcome to frame the purpose and relevance of Listenings 1 and 2. Ask: *What did you learn from Listenings 1 and 2 that will help you interview a group about music?* (Students learned about the possible health benefits of music and the different kinds of music people like and why. They can use these ideas when preparing to interview their group.)

Vocabulary Skill: Using the dictionary
(5 minutes)

1. Direct students to read the information and the dictionary entry silently. Ask: *Which definition is "something that is good or helpful"? Which one has to do with work?*

2. Check comprehension: *Why is definition 1 the best definition for this sentence?*

Skill Note

Point out that the sample sentences and the information about part of speech in the dictionary can be very useful in determining which word definition is the right one.

Critical Thinking Tip (1 minute)

1. Read the tip aloud.

2. Remind students that they will occasionally come across a word they don't know. Determining the meaning of the word based on context will help them in these instances.

A (5 minutes)

Direct students to work individually to read the sentences and dictionary entries and choose the correct definitions.

> **Activity A Answers, pp. 132-133**
> **1.** 2;
> **2.** 1;
> **3.** 3;
> **4.** 1;
> **5.** 3

B (10 minutes)

1. Have partners compare answers.

2. Go over the answers as a class. Elicit the context clues in the sentences that helped students choose the correct meaning.

> **MULTILEVEL OPTION**
>
> Seat lower-level students together and help this group complete the activity. While you are working with lower-level students, ask higher-level students to choose one or two of the words from Activity A and write a sentence using another definition.

CD2, Track 36

1. Direct students to work with a partner to read the excerpts and guess what the missing gerunds will be. Tell them not to write the words in until they listen to the audio.

2. Play the audio and ask students to complete the excerpts.

3. Go over the answers as a class.

> **Activity A Answers, pp. 134–135**
> **1.** Listening, Dancing;
> **2.** playing, Writing, playing;
> **3.** Singing, spending, singing;
> **4.** taking, Hearing

▶ *Listening and Speaking 1, page 135*

B (10 minutes)

Direct students to work individually to write the sentences.

> **Activity B Answers, p. 135**
> Possible sentences:
> **1.** Hearing my favorite song makes me happy.
> **2.** I enjoy listening to music in the morning.
> **3.** Singing with my friends is fun.
> **4.** Dancing is good exercise.
> **5.** Playing an instrument is satisfying.

C (10 minutes)

1. Ask students to take turns reading their sentences with a partner.

2. Call on volunteers to write sentences on the board. Correct them together, focusing on the use of gerunds.

 For additional practice with gerunds as subjects or objects, have students visit *Q Online Practice*.

MULTILEVEL OPTION

Seat students in mixed-ability pairs. Direct them to come up with the sentences orally before writing them down. Ask the higher-level students to assist their lower-level classmates with spelling and grammar.

Critical Q: Expansion Activity

Determining the Correct Definition

Take students through the process of choosing a correct definition by looking at context. Have them look at sentence 2 in Activity A. Point out that the words *people don't play that kind of music anywhere else* provide a good clue to what *special* means in that sentence. Ask students what these words are implying (that the music is not usual or ordinary).

Direct students to look up the word *tune* in their dictionaries. Ask them which definition and part of speech they have been using in this unit. Point out that how the word is used completely changes depending on whether the word is a verb or a noun. Do the same with *note* and *pop*.

 For additional practice with guessing the meaning of words from context, have students visit *Q Online Practice*.

▶ *Listening and Speaking 1, page 134*

SPEAKING

Grammar: Gerunds as subjects or objects (10 minutes)

1. Read the information about gerunds as subjects.

2. Check comprehension by writing several gerund "subjects" on the board (*Walking ___, Exercising ___, Learning English ___*) and eliciting sentence completions (*is good for you, is difficult, is fun*).

3. Ask: *Is a gerund a noun or a verb?*

4. Read the information about gerunds as objects.

5. Check comprehension by writing *I like ___* and *I don't like ___* on the board and eliciting sentence completions.

Skill Note

Students may confuse gerunds with present continuous verbs. Write a mixture of present continuous sentences and gerund as subject or object sentences on the board and have students identify the *-ing* form. For example, *He is listening to music. Listening to music is relaxing. I love listening to music.* Point out that when the *-ing* form is part of a verb, it's always preceded by a form of *be*.

Pronunciation: Intonation in questions of choice (5 minutes)

CD2, Track 37

1. Read the information about intonation and play the audio examples.
2. Have students repeat the questions.
3. Check comprehension. *Does your voice rise or fall on the first choice? On the second choice?*

Skill Note

Intonation is often an important clue for the listener. In this case it's a clue that a choice is coming. Have students practice using items on their desks with questions of choice. *Do you want the pencil or the pen? Would you like the book or the dictionary?* As they practice, monitor and provide feedback on intonation.

Listening and Speaking 1, page 136

A (5 minutes)

CD2, Track 38

1. Have students read the sentences and check the questions of choice.
2. Play the audio and ask students to repeat the questions.

Activity A Answers, p. 136
Checked: 1, 4, 5, 7, 8

B (5 minutes)

1. Have students ask and answer the questions with a partner.
2. Monitor and provide feedback on pronunciation.

web For additional practice with intonation in questions of choice, have students visit *Q Online Practice*.

Speaking Skill: Asking for and giving opinions (5 minutes)

1. Direct students to read the information about asking for and giving opinions.
2. Check comprehension by calling on individuals to ask for and give opinions about music by using the expressions.

21ST CENTURY SKILLS

Employers are always looking for employees who are team players, and one of the basics of working well with others is being able to share opinions. In a collaborative workplace, being able to ask others for their opinions is as important as being able to politely express your own. Teaching students how to ask for and give opinions establishes the foundation they need to politely share ideas.

Point out to students that in team-oriented work and study environments, it's important to get the contributions of every member of the team so that everyone's strengths and talents can benefit the group. Students (or workers) who don't solicit the opinions of others may be seen as disinterested.

Listening and Speaking 1, page 137

A (10 minutes)

1. Direct students to read the topics in the box.
2. Ask them to write questions about three of the topics using the phrases from the skill box on page 136.
3. Monitor and provide feedback on the questions.

Activity A Answers, p. 137
Possible answers: What do you think of Mozart? How do you feel about pop music? Do you think folk dancing is interesting?

MULTILEVEL OPTION

Ask higher-level students to write questions for all of the topics.

B (5 minutes)

Have students ask and answer the questions from Activity A with their partners.

web For additional practice with asking for and giving opinions, have students visit *Q Online Practice*.

Q Unit Assignment: Interview a group about musical preferences

Unit Question (5 minutes)

Refer students back to the ideas they discussed at the beginning of the unit about why music is important to them. Cue students if necessary by asking specific questions about the content of the unit: *What benefits of music did we learn about? Why was music important to the people in the second listening?*

Learning Outcome

1. Tie the Unit Assignment to the unit learning outcome. Say: *The outcome for this unit is to participate in a group interview about how important music is in your lives. This Unit Assignment will allow you to use gerunds as subjects or objects, pronounce questions of choice correctly, and ask for and give opinions.*

2. Explain that you are going to use a rubric similar to their Self-Assessment checklist on p. 138 to grade their Unit Assignment. You can also share a copy of the Unit Assignment Rubric (on p. 77 of this *Teacher's Handbook)* with the students.

Consider the Ideas (5 minutes)

CD2, Track 39

1. Direct students to read the questions before they listen.

2. Play the audio and have them check the questions they hear.

3. Call on volunteers to read the questions they heard aloud.

> **Consider the Ideas Answers, p. 137**
> Checked: b, c, f

▶ *Listening and Speaking 1, page 138*

Prepare and Speak

Gather Ideas

A (10 minutes)

1. Group students and tell them to look over the topics and brainstorm questions. Remind them to use the phrases from the skill box on page 136.

2. While students are working, monitor and encourage them to be creative and specific with their questions.

Organize Ideas

B (10 minutes)

1. Have students work with the same group from Activity A. Read the directions and direct students to look at the sample chart on p. 124.

2. Check understanding of the activity: *How many columns should you make in the chart? What do you write in the chart? Does everyone choose different questions or should every student in the group write the same five questions?*

3. Tell students to choose the questions they think will yield the most interesting answers. Tell them they will be interviewing several people, so they should leave enough space in the chart for three or four answers.

4. Monitor and provide feedback while students are creating their interview charts.

Speak

C (15 minutes)

1. Direct students to look at the Self-Assessment checklist before they begin their interviews. Read the directions. Seat two groups together and demonstrate asking the first question of every interviewee and then having another group member ask the second question.

2. Have the groups conduct their interviews in front of the class and use the Unit Assignment Rubric on p. 77 of this *Teacher's Handbook* to score each student's performance in the interview.

3. Alternatively, give each student a Unit Assignment Rubric and assign an "evaluee" for him or her to pay special attention to during the activity. Have them complete the rubric for that person.

Alternative Unit Assignments

Assign or have students choose one of these assignments to do instead of, or in addition to, the Unit Assignment.

1. Research your favorite singer and give an oral presentation about him or her. Where is he or she from? What is his or her music like?

2. Choose a song you like in English. Then find the lyrics (words) online. Study the lyrics. What do you think the song is about? Why do you like this song? Tell the class. Play the song if you have it.

For an additional unit assignment, have students visit *Q Online Practice*.

Check and Reflect

Check

A (5 minutes)

1. Direct students to read and complete the Self-Assessment checklist.

2. Ask for a show of hands for how many students gave all or mostly *yes* answers.

3. Congratulate them on their success. Discuss the steps they can take if an item on the checklist was difficult for them. For example, if they had trouble using intonation in questions of choice, they should listen again to the examples on p. 135 and practice repeating them.

▶ *Listening and Speaking 1, page 139*

Reflect

B (5 minutes)

1. Refer students to the learning outcome on p. 139. Tell them to talk with their partners about whether they achieved the learning outcome.

2. Elicit the answers to the Unit Question that students came up with at the beginning of the unit.

3. Encourage them to flip through the unit as they discuss the new things they learned and new answers they may have to the Unit Question.

Track Your Success (5 minutes)

1. Have students circle the words they have learned in this unit. Suggest that students go back through the unit to review any words they have forgotten.

2. Have students check the skills they have mastered. If students need more practice to feel confident about their proficiency in a skill, point out the page numbers and encourage them to review.

3. Read the learning outcome aloud. Ask students if they feel that they have met the outcome.

Unit Assignment Rubric

Student name: _____

Date: _____

Unit Assignment: *Interview a group about musical preferences.*

20 points = Interview element was completely successful (at least 90% of the time).
15 points = Interview element was mostly successful (at least 70% of the time).
10 points = Interview element was partially successful (at least 50% of the time).
 0 points = Interview element was not successful.

Interview a Group	20 points	15 points	10 points	0 points
Student spoke easily and clearly (without long pauses or reading) while asking and answering questions about music.				
Student used gerunds as subjects and objects correctly.				
Student used vocabulary from the unit.				
Student asked for and gave opinions.				
Student used correct intonation in questions of choice.				

Total points: _____

Comments:

LISTENING • making inferences
VOCABULARY • percentages and fractions
GRAMMAR • conjunctions *and* and *but*
PRONUNCIATION • linking consonants to vowels
SPEAKING • sourcing information

LEARNING OUTCOME

Conduct a survey to gather opinions on honesty and dishonesty, and then report your results to the class.

▶ *Listening and Speaking 1, pages 140–141*

Preview the Unit

Learning Outcome

1. Ask for a volunteer to read the unit skills, then the unit learning outcome.

2. Explain: *This is what you are expected to be able to do by the unit's end. The learning outcome explains how you are going to be evaluated. With this outcome in mind, you should focus on learning these skills (Listening, Vocabulary, Grammar, Pronunciation, Speaking) that will support your goal of conducting a survey on honesty/dishonesty and reporting your results for the class. This can also help you act as mentors in the classroom to help the other students meet this outcome.*

A (10 minutes)

1. Prepare students for thinking about the topic by asking questions about honesty. *What is honesty? Is it always good to be honest?*

2. Put students in pairs or small groups to discuss the first two questions.

3. Call on volunteers to share their ideas with the class. List their examples of honest and dishonest actions on the board.

4. Focus students' attention on the photo. Have a volunteer describe the photo to the class. Ask: *Where is the student?* Read the third question aloud. Elicit answers from volunteers.

Activity A Answers, p. 141
Possible answers:
1. tell the truth, confess wrongdoing, return found money, tell cashier when they're undercharged;
2. lie, steal, cheat;
3. The student is being dishonest because he's breaking a classroom rule or possibly cheating on a test. The student is not being dishonest—maybe he is receiving an important message.

B (15 minutes)

1. Read the Unit Question aloud: *When is honesty important?* Point out that answers to the question can fall into categories: *Personal Relationships, Work,* and *School.*

2. Write each category at the top of a sheet of poster paper. Give students a minute to silently consider their answers to the question.

3. Elicit answers to the question and make notes of the answers under the correct category.

4. Post the lists to refer to later in the unit.

Activity B Answers, p. 141
Possible answers: Lower-level students may give short answers: *always, at school, at work, with friends;* Mid-level students may be more specific: Work: *important not to steal, to report hours worked correctly, not to lie about absences or lateness;* School: *important not to copy from friends, not to plagiarize, not to cheat on tests;* Personal Relationships: *important to tell friends if they're making a mistake, to be honest about feelings.* Higher-level students may provide an anecdote to illustrate their opinions: *My co-worker was dishonest, and no one at work respected him.*

The Q Classroom
🔊 CD3, Track 2

1. Play The Q Classroom. Use the example from the audio to help students continue the conversation.

2. Ask: *How did the students answer the question? Do you agree or disagree with their ideas? Why?*

▶ *Listening and Speaking 1, page 142*

C (10 minutes)

Direct students to read the directions and complete the survey individually.

Critical Thinking Tip (1 minute)

1. Read the tip aloud.

2. Remind students that they will often be required to judge choices and decisions as well as actions.

Critical Q: Expansion Activity ●●●●●●●

Making Judgements and Providing Reasons

Explain to students that in most circumstances in life when they make a judgment, they'll have to support it with reasons. Ask students to consider their reasons behind the judgements they made about the actions in the survey. *Why is it very/not very wrong? Does this action harm someone? Does it have long-term consequences?* Have volunteers give their reasons for each choice in the survey as they do Activity D.

D (10 minutes)

1. Have partners share their opinions about the actions on the survey. Remind students to support their opinions with reasons.

2. Elicit the students' opinions and find out where there was agreement and disagreement.

EXPANSION ACTIVITY: Add to the Survey
(10 minutes)

1. Put students into small groups.

2. Ask students to come up with three additional items for the survey. Tell them the items can concern honesty at work, at school, or in their personal lives.

3. Have the group members ask students from other groups for their responses to the new items.

LISTENING

▶ *Listening and Speaking 1, page 143*

LISTENING 1: Dishonesty in Schools

VOCABULARY (15 minutes)

1. Direct students to read the sentences and write the bold words next to the correct definitions. Remind them to look for context clues.

2. Elicit the answers and have students repeat the bold words.

MULTILEVEL OPTION

Group lower-level students and assist them with the task. Provide alternate example sentences to help them understand the words. For example: *The **survey** had a lot of questions. **According** to my mother, I don't eat enough.*

Assign one word to each higher-level student and ask him or her to write a sentence with it. Have the higher-level students put their sentences on the board. Correct the sentences with the whole class, focusing on the use of the words rather than other grammatical issues.

Vocabulary Answers, p. 143
a. grade; **b.** cheat; **c.** survey;
d. technology; **e.** a quarter; **f.** suffer;
g. according to; **h.** prevent

 For additional practice with the vocabulary, have students visit *Q Online Practice*.

▶ *Listening and Speaking 1, page 144*

PREVIEW LISTENING 1 (5 minutes)

1. Direct students to look at the photo. Ask: *What is the student doing?*

2. Read the introduction and the answer choices aloud. Have students check their answers.

3. Tell students they should review their answers after the listening.

Preview Listening 1 Answer, p. 144
Checked: 75%

Listening 1 Background Note

Increased pressure to succeed combined with access to technologies that make cheating easier has led to an increase in cheating around the world. Some schools are fighting cheating by banning electronic technologies, and many teachers require students to turn in essays and reports to a website where they can be scanned for plagiarism.

However, many people feel that the cheating problem needs to be addressed in the curriculum and in the culture of the school, by having discussions with students about why cheating is wrong and making an all-out effort to create an environment where cheating is unacceptable. Others suggest that teachers should deter cheating by creating more exams that require students to explain their thought processes and having fewer tests based simply on the recall of facts.

LISTEN FOR MAIN IDEAS (5 minutes)

 CD3, Track 3

A (5 minutes)

1. Ask students to read the paragraphs.
2. Play the audio and have students complete the activity individually.
3. Elicit the answer from the class.

> **Listen for Main Ideas Answers, p. 144**
> Checked: 2

LISTEN FOR DETAILS (10 minutes)

 CD3, Track 4

1. Direct students to read the sentences.
2. As you play the audio, have students circle the correct words to complete the sentences.
3. Call on volunteers to read the completed sentences to the class.

> **Listen for Details Answers, p. 144**
> **1.** high school;   **2.** more than;   **3.** high school;
> **4.** send messages;   **5.** impossible;   **6.** Europe

 For additional practice with listening comprehension, have students visit *Q Online Practice*.

▶ *Listening and Speaking 1, page 145*

WHAT DO YOU THINK? (10 minutes)

1. Ask students to read the questions and reflect on their answers.
2. Seat students in small groups and assign roles: a group leader to make sure everyone contributes, a note-taker to record the group's ideas, a reporter to share the group's ideas with the class, and a timekeeper to watch the clock.
3. Give students five minutes to discuss the questions. Call time if conversations are winding down. Allow them an extra minute or two if necessary.
4. Call on each group's reporter to share ideas with the class.

> **What Do You Think? Answers, p. 145**
> **1.** Students are hurting themselves; they are missing a chance to learn something interesting; they need to learn that school isn't just about grades—they should study and work hard;
> **2.** Possible answers: Cheating is a problem because students will pass courses without learning the material. Cheating isn't a problem because most students only cheat on things that don't really matter.
> **3.** Possible answers: No, because students are creative, and if they want to cheat, they will find a way to do it.

Learning Outcome

Use the learning outcome to frame the purpose and relevance of Listening 1. Ask: *What did you learn from Listening 1 that will help you conduct a survey about honesty and dishonesty?* (Students learned some statistics about cheating in schools as well as different ways students cheat. They can use some of this information when conducting their survey.)

Listening Skill: Making inferences
(5 minutes)

1. Direct students to read the information about making an inference.
2. Check comprehension by asking questions: *What do you do when you make an inference? Why can we make the inference that Wendy Smith is upset about her students' cheating?*

A (5 minutes)

 CD3, Track 5

1. Direct students to read the answer choices, which are inferences about each person.

2. Play the audio and ask students to circle the correct inference. Tell them to pay attention to the context and listen for tone of voice.

> **Activity A Answers, p. 145**
> **1.** a;   **2.** b;   **3.** b;   **4.** a;   **5.** a

 Listening and Speaking 1, page 146

B (5 minutes)

1. Direct students to compare answers with a partner.

2. Replay the audio. Have pairs discuss the information in the audio that helped them get the answers.

> **Activity B Answers, p. 146**
> **1.** "I think it's all the new technology."
> **2.** "Don't they know they are only hurting themselves?"
> **3.** "I think my students are honest."
> **4.** "I don't think we need anything like that. It's a waste of time and money."
> **5.** "Actually, I think cameras are a *good* idea."

 For additional practice with making inferences, have students visit *Q Online Practice*.

LISTENING 2:
What's the Right Thing to Do?

VOCABULARY (10 minutes)

1. Direct students to read the sentences and definition choices.

2. Ask students to circle the definitions that match the bold words. Remind them to look for context clues.

3. Elicit the answers and have students repeat the bold words.

> **Vocabulary Answers, pp. 146–147**
> **1.** b;   **2.** a;   **3.** a;   **4.** b;   **5.** a;   **6.** a;   **7.** b;   **8.** a

 For additional practice with the vocabulary, have students visit *Q Online Practice*.

▶ *Listening and Speaking 1, page 147*
PREVIEW LISTENING 2 (5 minutes)

1. Direct students' attention to the photo and ask: *What do you think is happening in this photo?*

2. Have students read the introduction and write an idea next to each situation.

3. Tell students they should revisit their answers after they listen.

> **Preview Listening 2 Answers, p. 147**
> Possible answers: At school: copying homework, copying from the Internet; Getting a job: lying about job experience, using false references; Using the Internet: stealing movies or music, copying photos or other work without permission

LISTEN FOR MAIN IDEAS (5 minutes)

CD3, Track 6

1. Direct students to read the answer choices. Tell them they will circle one choice for each person.

2. Play the audio and have students complete the activity individually.

3. Call on volunteers for the answers.

> **Listen for Main Ideas Answers, p. 147**
> **1.** c;   **2.** b;   **3.** c

▶ *Listening and Speaking 1, page 148*
LISTEN FOR DETAILS (5 minutes)

CD3, Track 7

1. Direct students to read the statements and answer choices before they listen again.

2. As you play the audio, have students listen and circle their answers.

3. If necessary, replay the audio so that the students can check their answers.

4. Go over the answers with the class.

> **Listen for Details Answers, p. 148**
> **1.** c;   **2.** a;   **3.** a;   **4.** b;   **5.** a;   **6.** b

For additional practice with listening comprehension, have students visit *Q Online Practice*.

Q WHAT DO YOU THINK?

A (10 minutes)

1. Ask students to read the questions and reflect on their answers.

2. Seat students in small groups and assign roles: a group leader to make sure everyone contributes, a note-taker to record the group's ideas, a reporter to share the group's ideas with the class, and a timekeeper to watch the clock.

3. Give students five minutes to discuss the questions. Call time if conversations are winding down. Allow them an extra minute or two if necessary.

4. Call on each group's reporter to share ideas with the class.

> **Activity A Answers, p. 148**
> Possible answers:
> **1.** Copying a report or downloading music is wrong because you're stealing intellectual property. Giving false information on a resume is wrong because your boss will hire you without knowing your true abilities. (Students may also say that these actions are not wrong if they're not done to excess.)
> **2.** No, because you can hurt someone's feelings; Yes, because lying is always wrong.

B (5 minutes)

1. Have students continue working in their small groups to discuss the questions in Activity B. Tell them to choose a new leader, note-taker, reporter, and timekeeper.

2. Call on the new reporter to share the group's answers to the questions.

> **Activity B Answers, p. 149**
> Possible answers:
> **1.** People lie to protect their image, to make things easier for themselves, to protect others' feelings, to avoid confrontation, and for material gain.
> **2.** Students may agree with these statements and say that small lies (or white lies) don't really hurt anyone. Students may disagree with these statements and say that people will appreciate being told the truth, or that succeeding honestly might take more work, but is more fulfilling.

Learning Outcome

Use the learning outcome to frame the purpose and relevance of Listenings 1 and 2 Ask: *What did*

you learn from Listenings 1 and 2 that prepares you to conduct a survey about honesty? (Students learned about different ways people are dishonest in school, at work, and in other areas of life. They can use this knowledge to expand their survey questions.)

Vocabulary Skill: Percentages and fractions (5 minutes)

1. Direct students to read the information about percentages and fractions.

2. Check comprehension: *What fraction is twenty-five percent? What percentage is one-third?*

Skill Note

In everyday conversation, we usually use fractions when discussing physical things: *She drank half the coffee; A quarter of the students are from Korea.* It's more common to use percentages when talking about prices and numbers: *The shoes are 25% off; He got 90% of the answers correct.* Percentages are also used when more precise numbers are needed: *Twenty-three percent of the population* vs. *Around a quarter of the population.*

▶ *Listening and Speaking 1, page 150*

A (5 minutes)

 CD3, Track 8

1. Direct students to read the excerpts before they listen.

2. As you play the audio, have students write the correct percentage or fraction. Emphasize that they should write words rather than numbers.

3. Go over the answers with the class.

> **Activity A Answers, p. 150**
> **1.** seventy-five percent, half;
> **2.** a quarter;
> **3.** twenty-five percent;
> **4.** a third

B (10 minutes)

1. Have students work individually to write the numbers.

2. Ask volunteers to write the numbers on the board.

> **Activity B Answers, p. 150**
> **1.** 75%, ½; **2.** ¼; **3.** 25%; **4.** ⅓

 For additional practice with percentages and fractions, have students visit *Q Online Practice.*

▶ *Listening and Speaking 1, page 151*

SPEAKING

Grammar: Conjunctions *and* and *but*
(5 minutes)

1. Read the information about using *and* and *but*. Draw students' attention to the punctuation, pointing out that the comma usually translates to a pause in speaking.

2. Check comprehension. Write a sentence with two possible endings on the board: *She cheated on her test—she got caught/she failed it anyway.*

3. Ask students to connect the second part to the first using *and* or *but*.

Skill Note

But and *and* are coordinating conjunctions which combine two independent clauses. A comma should be used before the conjunction. The complete set of coordinating conjunctions is *for, and, nor, but, or, yet, so* (FANBOYS), but at this level, students will probably only use *and, but, or,* and *so.*

A (10 minutes)

1. Direct students to work individually to complete the sentences with *and* or *but.*

2. Have partners take turns reading the sentences.

3. Ask volunteers to read the sentences aloud.

> **Activity A Answers, pp. 151–152**
> **1.** but;   **2.** and;   **3.** but, and;   **4.** but, and;
> **5.** but;   **6.** and;   **7.** and, but;   **8.** and

▶ *Listening and Speaking 1, page 152*

B (10 minutes)

1. Direct students to work individually to circle the conjunctions complete the sentences.

2. Monitor and provide assistance as necessary.

> **Activity B Answers, p. 152**
> Possible answers:
> **2.** but he's really thirty.
> **3.** and I took it to the police.
> **4.** but it's illegal.
> **5.** and he copied it.
> **6.** but no one ever found out.

C (10 minutes)

1. Have partners read their sentences together.

2. Ask volunteers to write sentences on the board. Correct them together, focusing on the use of *and* and *but.*

 For additional practice with the conjunctions *and* and *but,* have students visit *Q Online Practice.*

Pronunciation: Linking consonants to vowels (5 minutes)

🔊 CD3, Track 9

1. Read the information about linking. Play the audio and have students repeat the phrases.

2. If students are having trouble linking the words, try writing them on the board with the consonant attached to the second word, like this: *qui zanswers, fal sinformation.*

3. Have them repeat the phrases again.

Skill Note

Linking is an important part of producing fluid, natural-sounding English. Point out to students that although they will still be understood, if they do not use linking, their English will sound less fluent.

▶ *Listening and Speaking 1, page 153*

A (5 minutes)
🔊 CD3, Track 10

1. Have students look at the sentences and predict where they think linking will occur. Remind them to look for words that end in a consonant sound and are followed by words that begin with a vowel sound. Tell them not to draw the links until they listen.

2. Play the audio. Elicit the linked words and write them on the board.

3. Ask students to repeat the linked words.

Activity A Answers, p. 153

2. Is it; find in;

3. About a; quarter of; students in; cheated on;

4. call in;

5. Because of; musicians and; make as;

6. In our; an article.

B (10 minutes)

1. Have students take turns reading the sentences with a partner.

2. Monitor and provide feedback on linking.

 For additional practice with linking consonants to vowels, have students visit *Q Online Practice*.

Speaking Skill: Sourcing information

(5 minutes)

1. Direct students to read the information about referring to sources.

2. Check comprehension. Write the beginning of each phrase on the board: *According to, The survey, The results*, etc.

3. Have students close their books or cover the page.

4. Elicit statements with the phrases on the board, asking students to use any information they remember from the listening activities.

21ST CENTURY SKILLS

Referring correctly to sources is a very important academic skill that is required for research papers and oral reports. However, students will also make use of this skill in future professional settings. When trying to be persuasive or show a solid foundation for one's thoughts, demonstrating background knowledge by sourcing information can make the difference between a weak and a strong argument.

▶ *Listening and Speaking 1, page 154*

A (10 minutes)

CD3, Track 11

1. Direct students to look at the magazine survey. Tell them to make guesses about the percentage of people who do the things listed.

2. Play the audio and have students check their answers.

Activity A Answers, p. 154

1. c;   **2.** b;   **3.** a;   **4.** e;   **5.** d

Tip for Success (1 minute)

1. Read the tip aloud. Emphasize that quotation marks should only be used with exact quotes, not with paraphrasing. Write two examples on the board:

According to the survey, a lot of students are cheating these days.

The article says, they share test answers, look at classmates' test papers, and send text messages with answers during a test.

2. Ask which sentence contains a word-for-word quote from the listening (the second) and where the quotation marks should go. Point out that the first word in a quote should begin with a capital letter.

B (10 minutes)

1. Have partners talk about the survey in Activity A using phrases from the skill box on page 153.

2. Ask volunteers to make statements about the survey for the class.

Activity B Answers, p. 154

Possible answers: The survey found that more than half of the people take paper or pens from their company to use at home; According to the survey, over ten percent of people sometimes change the price tag to a lower price for something they want to buy; The results showed that about 20% of people give false information on a resume.

 For additional practice with sourcing information, have students visit *Q Online Practice*.

▶ *Listening and Speaking 1, page 155*

Unit Assignment: Report on a class survey

Unit Question (5 minutes)

Refer students back to the ideas they discussed at the beginning of the unit about when honesty is important. Cue students if necessary by asking specific questions about the content of the unit: *What are some dishonest actions we talked about? How did people feel about them?*

Learning Outcome

1. Tie the Unit Assignment to the unit learning outcome. Say: *The outcome for this unit is to conduct a survey about honesty/dishonesty and report your results to the class. This Unit Assignment is going to let you show your skill in using sentences with* and *and but and in giving sources for information.*

2. Explain that you are going to use a rubric similar to their Self-Assessment checklist on p. 156 to grade their Unit Assignment. You can also share a copy of the Unit Assignment Rubric (on p. 87 of this *Teacher's Handbook*) with the students.

Consider the Ideas (5 minutes)

CD3, Track 12

1. Direct students to read the survey results before they listen.

2. Play the audio and have them write the missing percentages.

3. Call on volunteers for the answers. Point out how Scott used various expressions to report his results and refer to the source of information (the survey).

4. Play the audio again and ask students to listen for these expressions.

> **Consider the Ideas Answers, p. 155**
> **1.** 62, 2
> **2.** 25, 75
> **3.** 10, 29; 0, 97; 25, 66

▶ *Listening and Speaking 1, page 156*

Prepare and Speak

Gather Ideas

A (10 minutes)

1. Elicit a few examples of *yes/no* and multiple choice questions. Then ask students to write five questions for their survey.

2. Explain that the purpose of asking a partner the questions at this point is to test the questions to see if there are any problems.

3. Write these questions on the board to help students evaluate their surveys. *Does your partner understand your questions? Does he/she think your answer choices make sense? Are all of your questions different (i.e., not asking for the same information with different words)?*

Organize Ideas

B (10 minutes)

1. Have students read the directions. Tell them the ten people should not include their original partner.

2. When students are ready to compile their results, elicit the percentages they might come up with, for example, 10 = 100%, 5 = 50%, 1 = 10%. Ask them to write the survey results as percentages.

Speak

C (10-15 minutes)

1. Direct students to look at the Self-Assessment checklist. Briefly review the phrases for sourcing information from p. 153 and the information about linking consonants to vowels on p. 152.

2. Group students and give each group member a copy of the Unit Assignment Rubric on p. 87 of this *Teacher's Handbook*. Have each student evaluate one other member of the group.

3. Alternatively, have the class listen as each student presents results and use the rubric to score each student's presentation.

> **MULTILEVEL OPTION**
>
> Allow lower-level students to refer to the phrases on page 153 when they present their survey results. After they present, have higher-level students share their opinions or analysis of what the results show.

Alternative Unit Assignments

Assign or have students choose one of these assignments to do instead of, or in addition to, the Unit Assignment.

1. Are there any traditional stories or sayings from your culture about the importance of honesty? Find out how to say them in English. Then make a poster with a picture and share it with the class.

2. Tell a story about a time when someone was dishonest with you. What happened? How did you feel? What did you do?

 For an additional unit assignment, have students visit *Q Online Practice*.

Check and Reflect

Check

A (5 minutes)

1. Direct students to read and complete the Self-Assessment checklist.

2. Ask for a show of hands for how many students gave all or mostly *yes* answers.

3. Congratulate them on their success. Discuss the steps they can take if an item on the checklist was difficult for them. For example, if they had trouble using vocabulary from the unit, they should go through the words in Track Your Success on p. 157, identify any words they aren't comfortable using, review the meanings and usage for those words, and try to use them in sentences.

Reflect

B (5 minutes)

1. Refer students to the learning outcome on p. 157. Tell them to talk with their partners about whether they achieved the learning outcome.

2. Elicit the answers to the Unit Question that students came up with at the beginning of the unit.

3. Encourage them to flip through the unit as they discuss the new things they learned and new answers they may have to the Unit Question.

▶ *Listening and Speaking 1, page 157*

Track Your Success (5 minutes)

1. Have students circle the words they have learned in this unit. Suggest that students go back through the unit to review any words they have forgotten.

2. Have students check the skills they have mastered. If students need more practice to feel confident about their proficiency in a skill, point out the page numbers and encourage them to review.

3. Read the learning outcome aloud. Ask students if they feel that they have met the outcome.

Unit Assignment Rubric

Student name: _____

Date: _____

Unit Assignment: *Report on a class survey.*

20 points = Presentation element was completely successful (at least 90% of the time).
15 points = Presentation element was mostly successful (at least 70% of the time).
10 points = Presentation element was partially successful (at least 50% of the time).
 0 points = Presentation element was not successful.

Report on a survey	20 points	15 points	10 points	0 points
Student spoke easily (without long pauses or reading) when presenting survey results and was easy to understand (spoke clearly and at a good speed).				
Student used *and* and *but* correctly.				
Student used vocabulary from the unit.				
Student used phrases to source information.				
Student correctly linked consonants to vowels.				

Total points: _____

Comments:

Unit QUESTION
Is it ever too late to change?

Life Changes

LISTENING • listening for different opinions
VOCABULARY • verb + noun collocations
GRAMMAR • imperative of *be* + adjective
PRONUNCIATION • content word stress in sentences
SPEAKING • checking for listeners' understanding

LEARNING OUTCOME

Deliver a presentation providing instructions on how a person can make a change in his/her life.

▶ *Listening and Speaking 1, pages 158-159*
Preview the Unit

Learning Outcome

1. Ask for a volunteer to read the unit skills, then the unit learning outcome.

2. Explain: *This is what you are expected to be able to do by the unit's end. The learning outcome explains how you are going to be evaluated. With this outcome in mind, you should focus on learning these skills (Listening, Vocabulary, Grammar, Pronunciation, Speaking) that will support your goal of providing instructions on how someone can make a change in his or her life. This can also help you act as mentors in the classroom to help the other students meet this outcome.*

A (10 minutes)

1. Prepare students for thinking about the topic by asking questions about change. *What are some life changes that people make? Is there a typical time of life to make those changes?*

2. Put students in pairs or small groups to discuss the first two questions.

3. Call on volunteers to share their ideas with the class. Elicit the reasons for their answers to the second question.

4. Focus students' attention on the photo. Have a volunteer describe the photo to the class. Ask: *Where are the people? What are they doing?*

5. Read the third question aloud. Elicit answers from volunteers.

Activity A Answers, p. 159
Possible answers:
1. I like change because it keeps things exciting. I don't like change because things are easier when they stay the same.
2. Young people find it easier because they are more flexible and more used to change. Older people find it easier because they are more mature and more able to handle change.
3. No, because it's harder to study and make changes when you're old. Yes, because she looks very happy.

B (15 minutes)

1. Read the Unit Question aloud. Give students a minute to silently consider their answers.

2. Write the Unit Question at the top of a sheet of poster paper. Add the sub-categories *Yes* and *No*.

3. Elicit students' answers and write them in the correct categories. Ask students to provide reasons for their answers and note them on the poster paper. Post the list to refer to later in the unit.

Activity B Answers, p. 159
Possible answers: Lower-level students may answer with a simple *Yes* or *No*. Mid-level students may add more detail: *No, because a person can always make changes. You can learn and keep your mind active. You can also improve your situation or your habits. Yes, because change becomes very difficult when you're older. You can lose what you have, and some changes are bad.* Higher-level students may supply anecdotes to illustrate their opinions: *My grandmother is learning English. Continuing to learn and change keeps her mind sharp.*

🔊 CD3, Track 13

1. Play The Q Classroom. Use the example from the audio to help students continue the conversation.

2. Ask: *How did the students answer the question? Do you agree or disagree with their ideas? Why?*

▶ *Listening and Speaking 1, page 160*

C (10 minutes)

1. Direct students to look at the chart and check the changes they've made in their lives. Ask them to write when it happened (the year and/or month, or how old they were at the time).

2. Take a quick vote to see how many students have experienced each change on the list.

3. Point out the commonalities among the students: *All of you have changed schools at some time.*

D (10 minutes)

1. Read the example and elicit possible endings: *It was a little difficult because…(I had to make new friends, I had to learn my way around, my new classes were more difficult).*

2. Have students tell a partner about their changes.

3. Call on volunteers to share something interesting they learned about their partners.

EXPANSION ACTIVITY: Follow-up Questions (15 minutes)

1. Tell students they are going to talk in more detail about one of the changes on the chart in Activity C. Ask them to choose the one they want to talk about and circle it.

2. Review the idea of follow-up questions (questions you ask when you want more information) and elicit follow-up questions for some of the items on the chart in Activity C. For example, *Where is your new home? Do you prefer your new home or your old home?*

3. Direct students to stand up with their books and find a partner. Have the partners ask each other follow-up questions about the circled event on their chart.

4. Tell them to find new partners when they've finished. Participate in the activity and assist students as needed.

5. Call time when everyone has had a chance to talk to several partners. Wrap up by eliciting anything interesting students learned about their classmates.

LISTENING

▶ *Listening and Speaking 1, page 161*

LISTENING 1: Attitudes about Change

VOCABULARY (15 minutes)

1. Direct students to read the words and definitions in the box.

2. Ask questions to help students connect with the new vocabulary: *What is an offer you **accepted** recently? What is something you **changed your mind** about? What part of learning English do you find **especially** difficult?* Pronounce and have students repeat the words.

3. Have students work with a partner to complete the sentences. Call on volunteers to read the completed sentences aloud.

4. Have pairs read the sentences together.

MULTILEVEL OPTION

Group lower-level students and assist them with the task as necessary.

Assign one word to each higher-level student and ask him or her to write a sentence with it. Have the higher-level students put their sentences on the board. Correct the sentences with the whole class, focusing on the use of the words or expressions rather than other grammatical issues.

Vocabulary Answers, pp. 161–162
1. accept;   **2.** especially;   **3.** opportunity;
4. progress;   **5.** flexible;   **6.** proverb;
7. change your mind;   **8.** remain

web➕ For additional practice with the vocabulary, have students visit *Q Online Practice.*

▶ *Listening and Speaking 1, page 162*

PREVIEW LISTENING 1 (5 minutes)

1. Direct students to look at the photo. Ask: *What life change does this photo represent?*

2. Have students read the introduction and match the proverbs to their meanings. Ask if they have any similar proverbs in their native languages.

   Preview Listening 1 Answers, p. 162
   1. b; **2.** c; **3.** a; **4.** d

Listening 1 Background Note

Some additional proverbs about change:

There is nothing permanent except change. Heraclitus, Greek philosopher (Meaning: Nothing stays the same, except the presence of change.)

A rolling stone gathers no moss. Proverb dating from the mid-14th century (Meaning: Someone who keeps changing and doesn't settle down doesn't acquire any lasting ties. Originally it had a negative meaning, but now it has a more positive association with freedom from restraints.)

Don't change horses in midstream. Popularized during Abraham Lincoln's campaign (Meaning: Don't change your leader or your methods when halfway through a task or project.)

The more things change, the more they stay the same. Translated from the French novelist Alphonse Karr, 1849 (Meaning: Nothing really changes—all change is on the surface.)

You must be the change you wish to see in the world. Mahatma Gandhi (Meaning: If you want the world to change, you must change your own behavior first.)

LISTEN FOR MAIN IDEAS (5 minutes)

 CD3, Track 14

A (5 minutes)

1. Ask students to read the sentences.
2. Play the audio and have students complete the activity individually.
3. Elicit the answer from the class.

   Listen for Main Ideas Answers, p. 162
   Checked: c

▶ *Listening and Speaking 1, page 163*
LISTEN FOR DETAILS (10 minutes)

 CD3, Track 15

1. Direct students to read the incomplete proverbs.
2. As you play the audio, have students complete the proverbs and write the country names.

3. Call on volunteers to read the proverbs and country names to the class.

   Listen for Details Answers, p. 163
   1. cat, dance, Morocco;
   2. does not, remains, Brazil;
   3. wise, never will, Spain;
   4. improve, different, Germany

 For additional practice with listening comprehension, have students visit *Q Online Practice.*

WHAT DO YOU THINK? (10 minutes)

1. Ask students to read the questions and reflect on their answers.
2. Seat students in small groups and assign roles: a group leader to make sure everyone contributes, a note-taker to record the group's ideas, a reporter to share the group's ideas with the class, and a timekeeper to watch the clock.
3. Give students five minutes to discuss the questions. Call time if conversations are winding down. Allow them an extra minute or two if necessary.
4. Call on each group's reporter to share ideas with the class.

   What Do You Think? Answers, p. 163
   Possible answers:
   1. Students may like the proverb that they believe to be most true, or they may like a proverb that's similar to one in their own country.
   2. that you have to accept change, not be afraid to take the first step, and be flexible;
   3. Students may say that change is viewed as a positive thing in their cultures or that people of certain ages in their cultures are very open to change; or they may say that their cultures are more traditional and view change as a negative thing.

Tip for Success (5 minutes)

1. Read the tip aloud. Share with students other common English proverbs.
2. Explain that while they don't want to use proverbs constantly, knowing some can help them better understand natural, conversational English.

Learning Outcome

Use the learning outcome to frame the purpose and relevance of Listening 1. Ask: *What did you learn from Listening 1 that will help you deliver a presentation about how people can make a change in their lives?* (Students learned that many cultures have proverbs and beliefs about change. They can use these ideas for their presentation.)

▶ *Listening and Speaking 1, page 164*

Listening Skill: Listening for different opinions (5 minutes)

1. Direct students to read the information about expressions for agreeing and disagreeing.

2. Have students repeat the example expressions. Emphasize the importance of learning the more polite (indirect) forms of disagreement. Explain that when we disagree, we often provide reasons for our opinion.

3. Check comprehension by making declarative statements and asking students to agree or disagree with you. *Chocolate is the best food in the world. Reading books is fun. Basketball is the most exciting sport.* Encourage students to provide reasons when they disagree.

A (5 minutes)

 CD3, Track 16

1. Direct students to read the conversations. Ask them to predict whether they will hear an expression of agreement or disagreement.

2. Play the audio and ask students to complete the conversations.

3. Call on volunteers to read the completed conversations aloud.

> **Activity A Answers, p. 163**
> **1.** I don't know about that;
> **2.** I totally agree;
> **3.** I'm not sure I agree;
> **4.** That's true

▶ *Listening and Speaking 1, page 165*

B (10 minutes)

1. Direct students to agree or disagree with the statements using the expressions from page 164.

2. Remind them to provide reasons for their opinions.

3. Provide feedback on use of the expressions.

 For additional practice with listening for different opinions, have students visit *Q Online Practice*.

> **MULTILEVEL OPTION**
>
> Group lower-level or less-verbal students. Make the statements and have the students take turns responding. Provide feedback on use of the expressions from p. 164.
>
> While you are working with lower-level students, ask higher-level students to work in small groups to plan a mini-debate on one of the statements. Each person should provide at least two reasons to support their opinion. Have volunteers perform their debates for the class.

▶ *Listening and Speaking 1, page 166*

LISTENING 2: Tips from a Life Coach

VOCABULARY (10 minutes)

1. Direct students to read the sentences and definition choices.

2. Ask them to circle the correct definition for each bold word. Remind them to look for context clues.

3. Elicit the answers and have students repeat the bold words.

> **Vocabulary Answers, p. 166**
> **1.** b; **2.** a: **3.** a; **4.** b; **5.** b; **6.** b; **7.** a; **8.** a

 For additional practice with the vocabulary, have students visit *Q Online Practice*.

▶ *Listening and Speaking 1, page 167*

PREVIEW LISTENING 2 (5 minutes)

1. Direct students' attention to the photo and ask: *What is this woman doing?*

2. Read the introduction and elicit responses to the preview question. Write students' ideas on the board to refer to after the listening.

Listening 2 Background Note

A life coach is a personal consultant who works with individuals to achieve specific goals. They are not psychologists or counselors and do not diagnose or treat mental health issues. They help people with their careers, families, relationships, and financial issues using methods that include weekly meetings, journal-writing, progress updates, and other strategies borrowed from the corporate world.

LISTEN FOR MAIN IDEAS (5 minutes)

🔊 CD3, Track 17

1. Direct students to read the three choices. Tell them to choose the one that best summarizes the radio show.

2. Play the audio and have students complete the activity individually.

3. Call on a volunteer for the answer.

> **Listen for Main Ideas Answers, p. 167**
> Checked: 3

LISTEN FOR DETAILS (5 minutes)

🔊 CD3, Track 18

1. Direct students to read the incomplete statements before they listen again.

2. As you play the audio, have students listen and complete the statements.

3. If necessary, replay the audio so that the students can check their answers.

4. Go over the answers with the class.

> **Listen for Details Answers, p. 167**
> **1.** small; **2.** Write down; **3.** goals; **4.** date;
> **5.** Celebrate

 For additional practice with listening comprehension, have students visit *Q Online Practice*.

▶ *Listening and Speaking 1, page 168*

Ⓠ WHAT DO YOU THINK?

A (10 minutes)

1. Ask students to read the questions and reflect on their answers.

2. Seat students in small groups and assign roles: a group leader to make sure everyone contributes, a note-taker to record the group's ideas, a reporter to share the group's ideas with the class, and a timekeeper to watch the clock.

3. Give students five minutes to discuss the questions. Call time if conversations are winding down. Allow them an extra minute or two if necessary.

4. Call on each group's reporter to share ideas with the class.

Activity A Answers, p. 168
Possible answers:

1. Habits could include health habits, study habits, social behavior, work habits, or physical habits (slouching, biting fingernails, etc.).

2. Yes. A life coach would be helpful because it's useful to get advice, report progress to someone, or get feedback; No. A friend is just as good as a life coach. Life coaches are expensive, and it's better to work out your own problems.

B (5 minutes)

1. Have students continue working in their small groups to discuss the questions in Activity B. Tell them to choose a new leader, note-taker, reporter, and timekeeper.

2. Call on the new reporter to share the group's answers to the questions.

Activity B Answers, p. 168
Possible answers:

1. Big changes make you feel nervous, worried, excited, insecure, homesick, tired, etc.

2. Students may say that they would like to get better grades, eat better, exercise more, or watch less TV.

Learning Outcome

Use the learning outcome to frame the purpose and relevance of Listenings 1 and 2. Ask: *What did you learn from Listenings 1 and 2 that prepares you to give a presentation about how someone can make life changes?* (Students learned views about change in different cultures and also how to facilitate important changes in their life. They can use this information in their presentations about making changes.)

▶ *Listening and Speaking 1, page 169*

Tip for Success (2 minutes)

1. Read the tip aloud. Show students an entry from a collocations dictionary (such as the *Oxford Collocations Dictionary for Students of English*) if you have one available.

2. Explain that a collocations dictionary can help them see which words are commonly used together (not just verb-noun combinations). For example, for the word *class*, they will find the adjectives *big, large, small, advanced, beginner's* and the verbs *give, take, teach, dismiss*.

Vocabulary Skill: Verb-noun collocations (5 minutes)

1. Direct students to read the information about verb-noun collocations.

2. Check comprehension: *What nouns go with* change? *What nouns go with* make? *What verbs go with* advice? *What verbs go with* goal?

Skill Note

Knowing collocations can help students better understand how a word is used. Although a collocations dictionary may be difficult for students of this level to use, it is an excellent tool for the teacher. When you teach a new vocabulary word, look it up in a collocations dictionary to see how it is most commonly used. Teach students the most important collocations for the new words they learn.

A (15 minutes)
🔊 CD3, Track 19

1. Direct students to read the excerpts and complete them with the missing collocations.

2. Play the audio and have students check their work.

3. Have students take turns reading the excerpts aloud with a partner.

> **Activity A Answers, pp. 169-170**
> **1.** attitudes; **2.** achieve; **3.** advice; **4.** mind;
> **5.** change; **6.** progress; **7.** advice; **8.** goals

▶ *Listening and Speaking 1, page 170*

B (10 minutes)

1. Refer students to the chart on p. 169 and elicit a sample question from a volunteer.

2. Have students work individually to write the questions. Monitor and provide feedback.

> **MULTILEVEL OPTION**
>
> Group lower-level students and assist this group. Elicit questions orally before students write. Allow everyone to write the same questions.
> For Activity C, partner lower- and higher-level students.

> **Activity B Answers, p. 170**
> Possible questions: Have you made any changes recently? Do you usually follow your parents' advice? What is a goal you want to achieve? Do you change your mind a lot? Do you want to change your attitude?

C (10 minutes)

1. Have partners ask and answer their questions.

2. Call on volunteer pairs to ask and answer questions for the class.

 For additional practice with verb-noun collocations, have students visit *Q Online Practice*.

▶ *Listening and Speaking 1, page 171*

SPEAKING

Grammar: Imperative of *be* with adjectives (5 minutes)

1. Read the information about using *be* + adjectives.

2. Check comprehension: *How do you give negative advice? What verb form can we use after many adjectives?*

3. Elicit an infinitive ending for *Be prepared.* For example: *Be prepared to take the exam.*

A (10 minutes)

1. Direct students to read the article and underline each example of *be* + adjective.

2. Call on volunteers for the answers.

> **Activity A Answers, p. 171**
> Underlined: Be sure; be ready; Be careful; Don't be afraid; Be prepared; Be flexible

▶ *Listening and Speaking 1, page 172*

B (10 minutes)

1. Model the activity with two volunteers. First play the life coach role. Then have a student play the life coach role.

2. Ask partners to take turns giving each other advice. Monitor and provide assistance as necessary.

C (10 minutes)

1. Elicit an example sentence from a volunteer. Have students work individually to write the sentences.

2. Have students share their sentences with a partner.

3. Ask volunteers to write sentences on the board.

4. Correct them together, focusing on the use of *be* + adjective.

> **Activity C Answers, p. 172**
> Possible sentences:
> Don't be afraid to speak; Be careful with your pronunciation; Be prepared to spend a long time learning the language; Be ready to correct your mistakes; Be sure to practice as much as possible.

 For additional practice with *be* + adjective, have students visit *Q Online Practice.*

Pronunciation: Content word stress in sentences (5 minutes)

CD3, Track 20

1. Read the information about content word stress.

2. Play the example sentences on the audio. Ask students to repeat the sentences.

3. Ask volunteers to say the sentences for the class. Provide feedback on content word stress.

Skill Note

Content words in sentences can be stressed by pronouncing them more loudly and at a higher pitch and by lengthening them. Help students identify and practice word stress by exaggerating. Say the sentences on page 172, first pronouncing the stressed words loudly, then pronouncing the stressed words at a higher pitch, and finally pronouncing them with exaggerated length. Have students repeat.

▶ *Listening and Speaking 1, page 173*

A (5 minutes)

CD3, Track 21

1. Have students read the sentences and circle the content words.

2. Play the audio. Elicit the stressed words and write them on the board.

> **Activity A Answers, p. 173**
> **1.** learn, change;   **2.** change, good, rest;   **3.** change, thoughts, change, world;   **4.** improve, change, perfect, change, often;   **5.** music, changes, dance;   **6.** change, life, changing, heart

B (10 minutes)

CD3, Track 22

1. Play the audio and have students repeat the proverbs.

2. Call on volunteers to say the proverbs for the class. Provide feedback on word stress.

3. Have students say the proverbs and discuss their meanings with a partner.

 For additional practice with content word stress in sentences, have students visit *Q Online Practice.*

Speaking Skill: Checking for listeners' understanding (5 minutes)

1. Direct students to read the information about checking for listeners' understanding.

2. Say and have students repeat the questions.

In the professional world, checking for understanding is a vital part of being a successful communicator. By learning to check for understanding, students can ensure that they are delivering their message with clarity and can identify anything they aren't explaining well. Additionally, checking for understanding eliminates miscommunication and ensures that everyone is on the same page, which is especially important in busy professional environments with no room for error. Whether learners are talking to classmates, co-workers, employers, or customers, a simple check for understanding will help them get their message across.

A (10 minutes)

1. Direct students to look back at Activity C on p. 172.

2. Tell them to look through their sentences and identify places where they can stop and check for understanding.

> **Activity A Answers, p. 173**
> Students will probably want to check for understanding between sentences.

Tip for Success (1 minute)

1. Read the tip aloud.

2. Have partners practice the expressions by asking one of their questions from Activity B on p. 170. Tell partners to respond with one of the expressions before giving a brief answer.

B (10 minutes)

1. Elicit some suggestions for being a better English student.

2. Seat students in groups and have them take turns giving instructions.

3. Monitor and provide feedback on how students are checking their listeners' understanding.

 For additional practice with checking for listeners' understanding, have students visit *Q Online Practice*.

▶ *Listening and Speaking 1, page 174*

Unit Assignment: Give instructions

Unit Question (5 minutes)

Refer students back to the ideas they discussed at the beginning of the unit about whether it's ever too late to change. Cue students if necessary by asking specific questions about the content of the unit: *What kinds of changes did we talk about? What advice did we hear about making changes?*

Learning Outcome

1. Tie the Unit Assignment to the unit learning outcome. Say: *The outcome for this unit is to give instructions on how to make a change in one's life. This Unit Assignment is going to let you show your skill in using collocations,* be + *adjectives, and appropriate content word stress.*

2. Explain that you are going to use a rubric similar to their Self-Assessment checklist on p. 176 to grade their Unit Assignment. You can also share a copy of the Unit Assignment Rubric (on p. 97 of this *Teacher's Handbook*) with the students.

Consider the Ideas (5 minutes)

◑ CD3, Track 23

1. Direct students to read the list of instructions before they listen. Play the audio and have them number the steps in order.

2. Elicit the answers from the class. Ask students what they think of this action plan for watching less TV. *Would you want to follow this plan?*

Consider the Ideas Answers, p. 174
1. Make a TV schedule.
2. Set a goal to watch less TV.
3. Write a list of other activities you like to do
4. Choose one or two hours when you usually…
5. Add one more activity into your schedule every week.
6. Celebrate when you achieve your goal.

▶ *Listening and Speaking 1, page 175*

Prepare and Speak

Gather Ideas

A (10 minutes)

1. Read through the list of topics and elicit examples of good habits, bad habits, personality traits, etc. Write the ideas on the board.

2. Elicit any other ideas students have and list those as well.

3. Direct students to look at Mei Ling's graphic organizer. Note that when she made this graphic organizer, she was just gathering ideas and hadn't yet put them in order. That step can come later.

4. Have students complete a graphic organizer in their notebooks. Monitor and provide feedback.

Critical Thinking Tip (1 minute)

1. Read the tip aloud.

2. Remind students that creativity will help them generate good ideas.

Critical Q: Expansion Activity

Generate Ideas

Point out how the graphic organizer helps with generating ideas. Show students how they can generate even more ideas around the outer boxes. For example, around *List other favorite activities,* they could write possible activities.

▶ *Listening and Speaking 1, page 176*

Organize Ideas

B (10 minutes)

1. Have students use the information in the graphic organizer they made to write the steps. Refer them to p. 171 as reminder of how to use *be* + adjective

2. Monitor and provide assistance as necessary.

Speak

C (10-15 minutes)

1. Direct students to look at the Self-Assessment checklist. Briefly review the phrases for checking for listeners' understanding from p. 173. Remind students about the importance of stressing content words.

2. Have students practice giving the instructions to a partner.

3. Ask partners to refer to the Self-Assessment checklist as they give each other feedback.

4. Group students and give each group member a copy of the Unit Assignment Rubric on p. 97 of this *Teacher's Handbook*. Have each student evaluate one other member of the group as he or she presents.

5. Alternatively, have the class listen as each student gives their instructions and use the rubric to score each student's presentation.

Alternative Unit Assignments

Assign or have students choose one of these assignments to do instead of, or in addition to, the Unit Assignment.

1. Draw a time line that shows the changes in your life. Be sure to include the dates for each change. Explain your time line to the class.

2. Compare how your country or city is now to how it was in the past. List some examples of changes. Then share the changes with a small group of classmates and say whether you think the changes are positive or negative.

 For an additional unit assignment, have students visit *Q Online Practice*.

Check and Reflect

Check

A (5 minutes)

1. Direct students to read and complete the Self-Assessment checklist.

2. Ask for a show of hands for how many students gave all or mostly *yes* answers.

3. Congratulate them on their success. Discuss the steps they can take if an item on the checklist was difficult for them. For example, if they had trouble checking for understanding, they could write the expressions down on note cards and review them before group discussions to remind themselves to use them during the discussion.

Reflect

B (5 minutes)

1. Refer students to the learning outcome on p. 177. Tell them to talk with their partners about whether they achieved the learning outcome.

2. Elicit the answers to the Unit Question that students came up with at the beginning of the unit.

3. Encourage them to flip through the unit as they discuss the new things they learned and new answers they may have to the Unit Question.

▶ *Listening and Speaking 1, page 177*

Track Your Success (5 minutes)

1. Have students circle the words they have learned in this unit. Suggest that students go back through the unit to review any words they have forgotten.

2. Have students check the skills they have mastered. If students need more practice to feel confident about their proficiency in a skill, point out the page numbers and encourage them to review.

3. Read the learning outcome aloud. Ask students if they feel that they have met the outcome.

Unit Assignment Rubric

Student name: _____

Date: _____

Unit Assignment: *Give instructions.*

20 points = Presentation element was completely successful (at least 90% of the time).
15 points = Presentation element was mostly successful (at least 70% of the time).
10 points = Presentation element was partially successful (at least 50% of the time).
 0 points = Presentation element was not successful.

Give Instructions	20 points	15 points	10 points	0 points
Student gave instructions on making a life change and spoke easily (without long pauses or reading) and clearly.				
Student used *be* + adjectives correctly.				
Student used vocabulary from the unit.				
Student checked for listeners' understanding.				
Student stressed content words in sentences.				

Total points: _____

Comments:

Unit QUESTION
When is it good to be afraid?

Fear

LISTENING • taking classification notes
VOCABULARY • idioms and expressions
GRAMMAR • *so* and *such* with adjectives
PRONUNCIATION • linking vowel sounds with /w/ or /y/
SPEAKING • expressing emotions

LEARNING OUTCOME

Use phrases for expressing emotions to describe a frightening experience.

▶ *Listening and Speaking 1, pages 178–179*

Preview the Unit

Learning Outcome

1. Ask for a volunteer to read the unit skills, then the unit learning outcome.

2. Explain: *This is what you are expected to be able to do by the unit's end. The learning outcome explains how you are going to be evaluated. With this outcome in mind, you should focus on learning these skills (Listening, Vocabulary, Grammar, Pronunciation, Speaking) that will support your goal of describing a frightening experience using phrases to express emotion. This can also help you act as mentors in the classroom to help the other students meet this outcome.*

A (10 minutes)

1. To get students thinking about the topic, elicit the name of a scary movie, a dangerous sport, and something that might be scary in everyday life.

2. Put students in pairs or small groups to discuss the first two questions.

3. Call on volunteers to share their ideas with the class. Ask for a show of hands. *How many people like scary movies? Roller coasters? Extreme sports?*

4. Focus students' attention on the photo. Have a volunteer describe the photo to the class. Ask: *Does that look fun? Would you do that?* Read the third question aloud. Elicit answers from volunteers.

Activity A Answers, p. 179
Possible answers:
1. insects, animals, hospitals, heights, enclosed spaces, crowds, amusement park rides, driving, deep water;
2. Students may say they enjoy the feeling of fear because it's exciting.
3. frightened, excited

B (15 minutes)

1. Introduce the Unit Question, *When is it good to be afraid?* Ask students to remember the fears they previously discussed with each other.

2. Elicit different fears and list them on a piece of poster paper.

3. Ask: *Is it good to be afraid of all of these things? When is it good to be afraid of these things? Which of these fears is resonable/unreasonable?*

Activity B Answers, p. 179
Possible answers: Lower-level students may give simple answers: *in dangerous places;* Mid-level students may give more detailed answers: *It is good to be afraid when your life is in danger.* Higher-level students may be able to explain their thinking: *Some people are afraid of flying, but it isn't good to be afraid because flying is actually very safe.*

The Q Classroom
◯) CD3, Track 24

1. Play The Q Classroom. Use the examples from the audio to help students continue the conversation. Ask: *How did the students answer the question? Do you agree or disagree with their ideas? Why?*

2. Ask if any of the students share Yuna's fears—spiders and airplanes.

C (10 minutes)

1. Direct students to look at the photos and check the fears they have.

2. Ask students to discuss their fears with their partners. Ask: *How bad is your fear? Do you avoid these things because you are afraid?*

D (10 minutes)

1. Direct students to copy the chart into their notebooks and then interview their classmates about what they are afraid of. Provide questions for students to use: *What is your worst fear? What else are you afraid of?*

2. Elicit students' fears, pointing out the most common and most unusual fears.

EXPANSION ACTIVITY: Scary Things (10 minutes)

1. Ask students to think of a scary movie, story, or amusement park ride they know about. Write some questions to guide them: (amusement park ride) *Where is it? What kind of "car" are you in? Why is it scary?* (story or movie) *What's it called? When did you see/read it? What happens? Why is it scary?* Tell them to think about but not write the answers to the questions.

2. Have students walk around the room, telling each other about the scary ride, story, or movie.

E (10 minutes)

1. Seat students in small groups and ask them to discuss the questions.

2. Call on individuals to share any interesting information that came up in their group discussions.

LISTENING

▶ *Listening and Speaking 1, page 181*

LISTENING 1: The Science of Fear

VOCABULARY (15 minutes)

1. Direct students to read the words and definitions in the box. Pronounce and have students repeat the words.

2. Have students work with a partner to complete the sentences.

3. Call on volunteers to read the completed sentences aloud.

4. Have pairs read the sentences together.

MULTILEVEL OPTION

Group lower-level students and assist them with the task. Provide alternate example sentences to help them understand the words. For example: *I feel **anxiety** when my son stays out late. When you **panic**, your heart beats very fast and you can't think clearly. Flying makes me nervous, but it's not a **phobia**—I still get on an airplane every summer.*

After higher-level students have completed the activity, tell the pairs to write a sentence for each word. Have volunteers write one of their sentences on the board. Correct the sentences with the whole class, focusing on the use of the words rather than other grammatical issues.

Vocabulary Answers, p. 181
1. strength; **2.** phobia; **3.** sweat; **4.** protect; **5.** get over; **6.** purpose; **7.** panic; **8.** anxiety

 For additional practice with the vocabulary, have students visit *Q Online Practice*.

▶ *Listening and Speaking 1, page 182*
PREVIEW LISTENING 1 (5 minutes)

1. Direct students to look at the photo. Ask: *How do you feel when you look at this picture?*

2. Read the introduction and the answer choices aloud. Have students check their answer.

3. Tell them they should review their answer after the listening.

Preview Listening 1 Answer, p. 182
Checked: It helps protect us from dangerous situations.

Listening 1 Background Note

Listening 1 mentions the most common phobias: those regarding spiders, snakes, high places, and small spaces. Some other common phobias include: dogs (often caused by being bitten by a dog during childhood), thunder and lightning, injections, social situations, flying, and germs or dirt.

English speakers also often use the word *phobia* to exaggerate a desire to avoid something: *He's got a dishwashing phobia.*

LISTEN FOR MAIN IDEAS (5 minutes)

CD3, Track 25

1. Ask students to read the statements.

2. Play the audio and have students mark the sentences *T* or *F*.

3. Elicit the answers from the class. Elicit corrections for the false sentences.

Listen for Main Ideas Answers, p. 182
1. F; **2.** T; **3.** F; **4.** T; **5.** T; **6.** F

LISTEN FOR DETAILS (10 minutes)

CD3, Track 26

1. Direct students to read the sentences before they listen again.

2. As you play the audio, have students listen and circle the correct words to complete the sentences.

3. Ask volunteers to read the completed sentences.

Listen for Details Answers, p. 182
1. different; **2.** money; **3.** strong;
4. phobias; **5.** make chemicals; **6.** warmer;
7. strong and tight; **8.** strength

web For additional practice with listening comprehension, have students visit *Q Online Practice*.

▶ *Listening and Speaking 1, page 183*

Q WHAT DO YOU THINK? (10 minutes)

1. Ask students to read the questions and reflect on their answers.

2. Seat students in small groups and assign roles: a group leader to make sure everyone contributes, a note-taker to record the group's ideas, and a reporter to share the group's ideas with the class, and a timekeeper to watch the clock.

3. Give students five minutes to discuss the questions. Call time if conversations are winding down. Allow them an extra minute or two if necessary.

4. Call on each group's reporter to share ideas with the class.

What Do You Think? Answers, p. 183
Possible answers:
1. Anxiety: money, work, relationships; Panic: during an accident or emergency; Phobia: animals, insects, small spaces;
2. race car driving, mountain climbing, downhill skiing, skateboarding

Learning Outcome

Use the learning outcome to frame the purpose and relevance of Listening 1. Ask: *What did you learn from Listening 1 that prepares you for describing a frightening experience?* (The lecturer explained what happens to your body when you feel fear. Students can use what they learned to help them describe how they felt during a frightening experience.)

Listening Skill: Taking classification notes (5 minutes)

1. Ask students to read the information about taking classification notes and look over the example.

2. Check comprehension by asking questions: *To take classification notes, what should you write first? What do you write in each category? How can you find the important points later?*

Tip for Success (1 minute)

1. Read the tip aloud.

2. Tell students they can sometimes use their textbooks to determine in advance how many categories they'll need in their notes.

▶ *Listening and Speaking 1, page 184*

A (5 minutes)

CD3, Track 27

1. Play the beginning of the audio and elicit the category the speaker will be talking about (*the effects of fear*). Have students write the category in their notebooks.

2. Continue the audio and have students note the main ideas in that category. Encourage them to use bullet points or numbers.

3. Call on volunteers to share what they wrote.

4. Give feedback on notetaking, reminding students that they don't need to write complete sentences.

Activity A Answers, p. 184
The effects of fear: 1. brain makes chemicals that cause physical reactions; 2. body gets warmer, sweat; 3. may hear or feel heart; heart beats faster; 4. body gets strong and tight; 5. may have extra strength

B (5 minutes)

 CD3, Track 28

1. Direct students to listen to the next part of the audio and take classification notes.
2. Tell them that this time they should have two categories.
3. Elicit the categories and the main ideas from volunteers.

Activity B Answers, p. 184
Category 1: Things people do because they want to feel fear: go on rides and roller coasters; drive fast cars and motorcycles; do adventure sports, e.g., skydiving and bungee jumping;
Category 2: Why some love fear and some don't: some brains send a message there's no real danger; other brains send a message that the fear is real.

MULTILEVEL OPTION

You may want to provide lower-level students with the two categories. Stop the audio after the discussion of each category to allow students to make notes. Then pair lower-level students with higher-level partners. Ask the higher-level students to explain their notes to the lower-level students.

 For additional practice with taking classification notes, have students visit *Q Online Practice*.

LISTENING 2: What Are You Afraid of?

Tip for Success (1 minute)

1. Read the tip aloud.
2. Tell students that if they wait longer than 24 hours, they are more likely to forget the original information, which will make it difficult to correct any information in their notes.

VOCABULARY (10 minutes)

1. Direct students to read the sentences and definition choices. Ask them to circle the correct definition for each bold word. Remind them to look for context clues.
2. Elicit the answers and have students repeat the bold words.

Vocabulary Answers, pp. 184–185
1. a; **2.** b; **3.** a; **4.** b; **5.** a; **6.** a; **7.** b **8.** a

 For additional practice with the vocabulary, have students visit *Q Online Practice*.

▶ *Listening and Speaking 1, page 185*

PREVIEW LISTENING 2 (5 minutes)

1. Direct students' attention to the photo and ask: *How does he feel?*
2. Read the introduction and elicit answers to the question.
3. Tell students to note down their own answer and revisit it once they have listened to the audio.

Listening 2 Background Note

Many people suffer from mild phobias that do not significantly disrupt their lives. However, people with strong phobias may require help from a doctor or therapist. The most common treatment, called "systematic desensitization," involves slowly exposing the patient to the object of fear in a sequence of steps. The patient first looks at or draws the feared object and then gets close to it. For example, someone with a fear of dentists might first just sit in the waiting room without going in for a treatment. Once the patient is comfortable with each step, the person moves on to the next step until he or she is completely participating in the feared activity.

LISTEN FOR MAIN IDEAS (5 minutes)

CD3, Track 29

1. Direct students to read the statements. Tell them they will check four reasons.
2. Play the audio and have students complete the activity individually.
3. Call on a volunteer for the answers.

Listen for Main Ideas Answers, p. 185
Checked: 1, 3, 4, 6

LISTEN FOR DETAILS (5 minutes)

🔊 CD3, Track 30

1. Direct students to read the questions and answer choices before they listen again.

2. As you play the audio, have students listen and circle the correct answers.

3. Have students compare answers with a partner.

4. Replay the audio so that the partners can check their answers.

5. Go over the answers with the class.

> **Listen for Details Answers, p. 186**
> **1.** a; **2.** b; **3.** c; **4.** c; **5.** a; **6.** a; **7.** b; **8.** c

 For additional practice with listening comprehension, have students visit *Q Online Practice*.

► *Listening and Speaking 1, page 187*

WHAT DO YOU THINK?

A (10 minutes)

1. Ask students to read the questions and reflect on their answers.

2. Seat students in small groups and assign roles: a group leader to make sure everyone contributes, a note-taker to record the group's ideas, a reporter to share the group's ideas with the class, and a timekeeper to watch the clock.

3. Give students five minutes to discuss the questions. Call time if conversations are winding down. Allow them an extra minute or two if necessary.

4. Call on each group's reporter to share ideas with the class.

> **Activity A Answers, p. 187**
> Possible answers:
> **1.** Yes, because the doctor is going to help her, and she wants to change; No, because her phobia is very extreme.
> **2.** Students may talk about a phobia that a friend or family member has, such as a fear of spiders. The person may be seeing a therapist or may be trying to get over it on their own.

B (5 minutes)

1. Have students continue working in their small groups to discuss the questions in Activity B. Tell them to take notes in the T-chart.

2. Call on individuals to share the group's answers to the questions. Create a class T-chart on the board.

> **Activity B Answers, p. 187**
> Possible answers:
> **1.** Ways fear can be good: it protects you from danger; it's exciting; Ways fear can be bad: it prevents you from doing things you want to; it interferes with your life.
> **2.** Some fears are reasonable and protect you from danger or prevent you from taking excessive risks; other fears are bad because they are unreasonable and they limit your opportunities in life.

Learning Outcome

Use the learning outcome to frame the purpose and relevance of Listenings 1 and 2. Ask: *What did you learn from Listenings 1 and 2 that will help you describe a frightening situation?* (Students learned what happens to people physically when they feel fear and how they can get over their fears. They can use what they have learned to describe how they felt during a frightening experience and what they did to get over their fear.)

Vocabulary Skill: Idioms and expressions (5 minutes)

1. Direct students to read the information silently.

2. Check comprehension: *What is an idiom or expression? Why is it important to learn them?*

Skill Note

The sheer number of idioms and expressions in English can be overwhelming for students. Advise them to learn idioms by noting down the ones they encounter, looking up their meanings, and paying attention to how they are used.

Point out that when it comes to using idioms, it's important that every word is correct—idioms cannot be approximate. For example, *Please get a seat* or *I'm completely ears* sounds very odd.

▶ *Listening and Speaking 1, page 188*

A (5 minutes)

1. Direct students to work with a partner to underline the idioms.
2. Go over the answers with the class.
3. Write the idioms on the board.

> **Activity A Answers, p. 188**
> **2.** can't stand
> **3.** you can say that again
> **4.** drives me crazy
> **5.** have a hard time;
> **6.** before you know it

B (10 minutes)

1. Have students work with their partners from Activity A to match the idioms and definitions.
2. Go over the answers as a class.
3. Provide unfinished questions and elicit completions from students: *He was so scared he was ___; A lot of people can't stand ___; ___ drives me crazy!; A lot of people have a hard time with ___; ___ is always over before you know it.*

> **Activity B Answers, p. 188**
> **1.** c; **2.** e; **3.** f; **4.** a; **5.** d; **6.** b

 For additional practice with idioms and expressions, have students visit *Q Online Practice*.

Tip for Success (3 minutes)

1. Read the tip aloud.
2. Have students look up some of the key words from the idioms on the page (*leaf, stand, crazy*) to see if the idioms are in their dictionaries.

▶ *Listening and Speaking 1, page 189*

SPEAKING

Grammar: *So* and *such* with adjectives
(5 minutes)

1. Read the information about using *so* and *such* for emphasis.
2. Check comprehension by asking questions: *Why do we use* so *or* such*? Which one do I use with a noun? Does* so *come before the adjective or after it?*

Skill Note

Although *so* and *such* are commonly used in speaking as synonyms for *very*, in writing they are often accompanied by a *that* clause showing result. *I was so scared that my hands were shaking. It was such a scary movie that I had nightmares.*

A (10 minutes)

1. Direct students to work individually to complete each sentence with *so* or *such*.
2. Call on volunteers to read the completed sentences aloud.

> **Activity A Answers, p. 189**
> **1.** so;
> **2.** such;
> **3.** so;
> **4.** so;
> **5.** such;
> **6.** such;
> **7.** so;
> **8.** such

B (10 minutes)

1. Direct students to work individually to write the sentences.
2. Call on volunteers to read their sentences.

> **Activity B Answers, p. 189**
> Possible sentences:
> **2.** It was such a big snake.
> **3.** It was such a scary movie.
> **4.** I am so afraid of public speaking.
> **5.** She is so worried.
> **6.** It was such a long flight.
> **7.** That was so loud.
> **8.** It is such an important test.

> **MULTILEVEL OPTION**
>
> Have higher-level students extend their sentences with a *that* clause: *I was so scared that I ran away.*

C (10 minutes)

1. Have students take turns reading their sentences aloud with a partner.
2. Ask volunteers to write their sentences on the board.

 For additional practice with *so* and *such* with adjectives, have students visit *Q Online Practice*.

Listening and Speaking 1, page 190

Pronunciation: Linking vowel sounds with /w/ or /y/ (5 minutes)

CD3, Track 31

1. Read the information about linking vowel sounds with /w/ and play the examples on the audio.

2. Have students repeat the examples. Provide more examples for them to practice with: *too easy, no exit, go in.*

3. Follow the same procedure with linking vowels with /y/ and provide additional examples: *he asked, free entry, why are.*

4. Check comprehension. Write word pairs on the board and ask students to identify which are linked with /y/ and which are linked with /w/: *who are, why is, so is, we are, you always.*

Skill Note

Point out to students that although they can be understood even if they don't link sounds correctly, linking is an important part of fluid, natural-sounding English. You may want to remind students of the other linking they practiced (consonants to vowels on p. 152).

A (5 minutes)

1. Have students read the sentences, underline the word pairs, and label the sentence with the correct linking sound.

> **Activity A Answers, pp. 190–191**
> **2.** Why are /y/;
> **3.** Julio is /w/;
> **4.** She always /y/;
> **5.** know anyone /w/;
> **6.** She is /y/;
> **7.** see anyone /y/;
> **8.** three other /y/

▶ *Listening and Speaking 1, page 191*

B (10 minutes)

CD3, Track 32

1. Play the audio and have students check their work. Go over the answers as a class.

2. Pair students and have them take turns reading their sentences aloud.

3. Monitor and provide feedback on pronunciation.

 For additional practice with linking vowel sounds with /y/ or /w/, have students visit *Q Online Practice.*

Speaking Skill: Expressing emotion (5 minutes)

1. Direct students to read the information about expressing emotion.

2. Have them repeat the example expressions.

3. Check comprehension: *Why should you express emotions when you are listening to others?*

21ST CENTURY SKILLS

"Interpersonal intelligence," or the ability to get along with and work well with others, is a highly valued skill in today's workplace. Tell students it's important they show that they value their colleagues and are interested in what they have to say. Knowing how to react appropriately when others are speaking will help students make a good impression and give them a tool they can use to relate to others.

A (10 minutes)

1. Direct students to read the conversations and circle the appropriate phrases.

2. Have them take turns reading the conversations aloud with a partner.

> **Activity A Answers, pp. 191–192**
> **1.** No kidding!
> **2.** I'm sorry to hear that.
> **3.** That's wonderful!
> **4.** How awful.
> **5.** No way!

▶ *Listening and Speaking 1, page 192*

B (10 minutes)

1. Direct students to work individually to complete the conversations.

2. Ask them to read the conversations with a partner.

3. Monitor and provide feedback on use of the expressions.

> **Activity B Answers, p. 192**
> Possible answers:
> **1.** Are you serious? I'm glad to hear that.
> **2.** How awful. That's wonderful.
> **3.** No kidding! That's terrible!

 For additional practice with expressing emotion, have students visit *Q Online Practice.*

Q Unit Assignment: Tell a personal story

Unit Question (5 minutes)

Refer students back to the ideas they discussed at the beginning of the unit about when it is good to be afraid. Cue them if necessary by asking specific questions about the content of the unit: *What kinds of fears did we talk about? Are any of these fears reasonable or unreasonable? How does the body respond to fear?*

Learning Outcome

1. Tie the Unit Assignment to the unit learning outcome. Say: *The outcome for this unit is to use phrases for expressing emotions to describe a frightening experience. This Unit Assignment is going to let you show that you've accomplished that outcome and that you can use* so *and* such *with adjectives and link vowel sounds.*

2. Explain that you are going to use a rubric similar to their Self-Assessment checklist on p. 194 to grade their Unit Assignment. You can also share a copy of the Unit Assignment Rubric (on p. 107 of this *Teacher's Handbook*) with the students.

Consider the Ideas (10 minutes)

🔊 CD3, Track 33

1. Direct students to read the chart headings. Play the audio and ask them to take notes in the chart.

2. Call on volunteers for the answers.

Consider the Ideas Answers, p. 193

When and where it happened	Who was there	What happened
summer after college; Green Mountains	Margo + her two best friends	They were sleeping and they heard a bear.
How I felt	What I did	How the story ended
scared	panicked	They turned on the radio and scared the bear away.

Prepare and Speak

Gather Ideas

A (10 minutes)

1. Direct students to think of three times in their life when they were afraid. To help other students get ideas, call on volunteers to briefly share their experiences.

2. While students are working, monitor and provide feedback on their note-taking. Remind them that they don't need to write complete sentences when they are taking notes.

Organize Ideas

B (10 minutes)

1. Have students choose one event from Activity A and make notes in the chart with their own information.

2. Monitor and provide feedback.

Critical Thinking Tip (1 minute)

1. Read the tip aloud.

2. Tell students that organizing ideas before speaking can make the difference between an average speech and an excellent speech.

Critical Q: Expansion Activity

Organize Ideas

Point out to students that while organizing their own ideas will make their stories easier for listeners to understand, it's also useful to organize the ideas they hear in order to improve their own understanding.

Have students copy the blank chart into their notebooks. Tell them to choose one classmate's story and complete the chart as they listen to the presentation.

Speak

C (10–15 minutes)

1. Direct students to look at the Self-Assessment checklist. Refer students to the vocabulary on pages 181 and 184, the use of *so* and *such* on p. 189, and the phrases for expressing emotion on p. 191.

2. Have students practice telling their stories to a partner. Ask partners to refer to the Self-Assessment checklist as they give each other feedback.

3. Put students into groups and give each group member a copy of the Unit Assignment Rubric on p. 107 of this *Teacher's Handbook*. Have each group member tell their story to the group. Remind students that they should respond to the person telling the story. Have each student evaluate one other member of the group. Point out that they need to evaluate the person as a speaker (when telling the story) as well as a listener.

4. Alternatively, have the class listen to each student's story, and use the rubric to score each student's storytelling and response skills.

Alternative Unit Assignments

Assign or have students choose one of these assignments to do instead of, or in addition to, the Unit Assignment.

1. Work with a partner. Think of a common phobia, such as a fear of snakes or a fear of closed spaces. Make a five-step plan to help someone get over the phobia. Share your plan with the class in a presentation.

2. Think about your dreams and nightmares. Make a list of scary things or events you have dreamed about. Then take a class poll to find out the top ten most common nightmares.

 For an additional unit assignment, have students visit *Q Online Practice*.

Check and Reflect

Check

A (5 minutes)

1. Direct students to read and complete the Self-Assessment checklist.

2. Ask for a show of hands for how many students gave all or mostly *yes* answers.

3. Congratulate them on their success. Discuss the steps they can take if an item on the checklist was difficult for them. For example, if they had trouble using *so* and *such*, they should review the grammar on pages 189-190 and on *Q Online Practice*.

Reflect

 B (5 minutes)

1. Refer students to the learning outcome on p. 195. Tell them to talk with their partners about whether they achieved the learning outcome.

2. Elicit the answers to the Unit Question that students came up with at the beginning of the unit.

3. Encourage them to flip through the unit as they discuss the new things they learned and new answers they may have to the Unit Question.

▶ *Listening and Speaking 1, page 195*

Track Your Success (5 minutes)

1. Have students circle the words they have learned in this unit. Suggest that students go back through the unit to review any words they have forgotten.

2. Have students check the skills they have mastered. If students need more practice to feel confident about their proficiency in a skill, point out the page numbers and encourage them to review.

3. Read the learning outcome aloud. Ask students if they feel that they have met the outcome.

Unit Assignment Rubric

Student name: _____

Date: _____

Unit Assignment: *Tell a personal story.*

20 points = Story element was completely successful (at least 90% of the time).
15 points = Story element was mostly successful (at least 70% of the time).
10 points = Story element was partially successful (at least 50% of the time).
 0 points = Story element was not successful.

Tell a Personal Story	20 points	15 points	10 points	0 points
Student told a story about a frightening experience and spoke easily (without long pauses or reading) and clearly.				
Student used *so* and *such* with adjectives.				
Student used vocabulary from the unit.				
Student reacted to others' stories by expressing surprise, happiness, or sadness.				
Student linked vowel sounds correctly.				

Total points: _____

Comments:

Welcome to the Q Testing Program

1. MINIMUM SYSTEM REQUIREMENTS[1]

1024 x 768 screen resolution displaying 32-bit color

Web browser[2]:
Windows®-requires Internet Explorer® 7 or above
Mac®-requires OS X v10.4 and Safari® 2.0 or above
Linux®-requires Mozilla® 1.7 or Firefox® 1.5.0.9 or above

To open and use the customizable tests you must have an application installed that will open and edit .doc files, such as Microsoft® Word® (97 or higher).

To view and print the Print-and-go Tests, you must have an application installed that will open and print .pdf files, such as Adobe® Acrobat® Reader (6.0 or higher).

2. RUNNING THE APPLICATION

Windows®/Mac®
- Ensure that no other applications are running.
- Insert the Q: Skills for Success Testing Program CD-ROM into your CD-ROM drive.
- Double click on the file "start.htm" to start.

Linux®
- Insert the Q: Skills for Success Testing Program CD-ROM into your CD-ROM drive.
- Mount the disk on to the desktop.
- Double click on the CD-ROM icon.
- Right click on the icon for the "start.htm" file and select to "open with Mozilla".

3. TECHNICAL SUPPORT

If you experience any problems with this CD-ROM, please check that your machine matches or exceeds the minimum system requirements in point 1 above and that you are following the steps outlined in point 2 above.

If this does not help, e-mail us with your query at: elt.cdsupport.uk@oup.com
Be sure to provide the following information:

- Operating system (e.g. Windows 2000, Service Pack 4)
- Application used to access content, and version number
- Amount of RAM
- Processor speed
- Description of error or problem
- Actions before error occurred
- Number of times the error has occurred
- Is the error repeatable?

---

[1] The Q Testing Program CD-ROM also plays its audio files in a conventional CD player.

[2] Note that when browsing the CD-ROM in your Web browser, you must have pop-up windows enabled in your Web browser settings.

The Q Testing Program

The disc on the inside back cover of this book contains both ready-made and customizable versions of **Reading and Writing** and **Listening and Speaking** tests. Each of the tests consists of multiple choice, fill-in-the-blanks/sentence completion, error correction, sentence reordering/sentence construction, and matching exercises.

Creating and Using Tests

1. Select "Reading and Writing Tests" or "Listening and Speaking Tests" from the main menu.
2. Select the appropriate unit test or cumulative test (placement, midterm, or final) from the left-hand column.
3. For ready-made tests, select a Print-and-go Test, Answer Key, and Audio Script (for Listening and Speaking tests).
4. To modify tests for your students, select a Customizable Test, Answer Key, and Audio Script (for Listening and Speaking tests). Save the file to your computer and edit the test using Microsoft Word or a compatible word processor.
5. For Listening and Speaking tests, use the audio tracks provided with the tests. **Audio files for the listening and speaking tests can also be played in a standard CD player.**

Reading and Writing Tests

Each test consists of 40 questions taken from the selected unit. The Reading and Writing Tests assess reading skills, vocabulary, vocabulary skills, grammar, and writing skills.

Listening and Speaking Tests

Each test consists of 40 questions taken from the selected unit. The Listening and Speaking Tests assess listening skills, vocabulary, vocabulary skills, grammar, pronunciation, and speaking skills.

Cumulative Tests

The placement tests for both Listening and Speaking and Reading and Writing consist of 50 questions. Each placement test places students in the correct level of Q: Introductory–5. **A printable User Guide to help you administer the placement test is included with the placement test files on the CD-ROM.**

The midterm tests for both Listening and Speaking and Reading and Writing consist of 25 questions covering Units 1–5 of the selected Level. The midterm Reading and Listening texts are new and not used in any other tests or student books.

The final tests for both Listening and Speaking and Reading and Writing consist of 25 questions covering Units 6–10 of the selected Level. The final Reading and Listening texts are new and not used in any other tests or student books.